*The Imperial Style:*
*Fashions of the*
*Hapsburg Era*

# The Imperial Style:
# Fashions of the
# Hapsburg Era

Based on the exhibition
Fashions of the Hapsburg Era:
Austria-Hungary
at The Metropolitan Museum of Art

December 1979–August 1980

The Metropolitan Museum of Art, New York
Distributed by Rizzoli, New York

The exhibition was made possible through grants from The
Edith C. Blum Foundation, B. Altman & Company, Henri
Bendel, Inc., Bergdorf Goodman, Bloomingdale's, Bonwit
Teller, Lord & Taylor, Saks Fifth Avenue-Gimbels Founda-
tion, and the Council of Fashion Designers of America.

Published by The Metropolitan Museum of Art, New York
Bradford D. Kelleher, Publisher
John P. O'Neill, Editor in Chief
Polly Cone, Editor
Doris L. Halle, Designer

On the jacket: Detail of a portrait of Empress Elisabeth. Oil on
canvas, 1865, by Franz Xaver Winterhalter. Hofburg, Vienna.

Frontispiece: Detail of a view of Vienna from the Belvedere. Oil
on canvas, 1759–60, by Bernardo Bellotto (called Canaletto).
Kunsthistorisches Museum, Vienna.

LIBRARY OF CONGRESS CATALOGING IN PUBLICATION DATA
Main entry under title:

The Imperial style.

   Bibliography: p.
   1. Costume—Austria—History—Addresses, essays,
lectures. 2. Costume—Hungary—History—Addresses,
essays, lectures. I. Cone, Polly. II. New York
(City). Metropolitan Museum of Art.
GT813.I46   391'.009436'07401471   80-11752
ISBN 0-87099-232-5
ISBN 0-8478-5322-5 (Rizzoli)

# Contents

# Foreword

During every one of the eight years that Diana Vreeland has been Special Consultant in the Costume Institute, the Museum has offered a grand exhibition of costumes, each one focusing on a different period, culture, or theme. I am happy to say that this delightful tradition continues, and that this year the Museum is proud to present *Fashions of the Hapsburg Era: Austria-Hungary.*

To correct what some men might term an imbalance, the current exhibition features many more men's costumes than have been shown in the past. This is especially apt in a show about the Hapsburg era—a time in which the magnificence of male dress was brilliantly demonstrated in the elegant court uniforms created for the nobility and their liveried servants. The exhibition also communicates the great range of styles seen at court in the vast Hapsburg Empire. The Austrian taste imparts a restrained elegance to the Viennese costumes in the show. In contrast, the Hungarian costumes vibrantly reflect the Magyar preference for rich colors and sumptuous materials and show the pronounced influence of oriental and Near Eastern opulence.

The exhibition is not only a delight to the eye, but also a magical means of transport to the past. The present publication supplies the reader with a more lasting guide to the vanished splendor so arrestingly captured in the show. The ten essays here, contributions from authorities in the field of costume and other writers conversant with life in Vienna and Budapest, convey the vitality, the high-pitched romanticism, and the courtly elegance that marked every facet of the Viennese and Hungarian societies.

Credit is due the editor of the book, Polly Cone, for her major role in shaping the publication. Helga Kessler, Lewisohn Fellow in the Costume Institute, was the translator of the chapters written in German and a constant source of aid and information for the editor. Stephen Jamail, of the Office of the Vice President for Operations, smoothed the way a hundred times with wit and flair. Mary Lorincz, of the Department of Twentieth Century Art, ably translated the chapter on Hungarian costume.

A special debt of gratitude goes to The Edith C. Blum Foundation, B. Altman & Company, Henri Bendel, Inc., Bergdorf Goodman, Bloomingdale's, Bonwit Teller, Lord & Taylor, Saks Fifth Avenue-Gimbels Foundation, and the Council of Fashion Designers of America, whose generous support made the exhibition possible.

Philippe de Montebello
Director
The Metropolitan Museum of Art

# Preface

The fashions worn during the Hapsburg era in Vienna and Budapest had their own kind of uniqueness. This is not to say that well-dressed Austrians and Hungarians of the periods covered in the exhibition were out of touch with what was considered fashionable in the rest of the western world. On the contrary, the upper-class Austrian and Hungarian ladies were well aware of the latest French fashions. The gentlemen, too, were very much in tune with the sartorial modes of the French in the eighteenth century, and later, in the nineteenth century, they turned to the English styles, with their accent on elegance and superb tailoring.

What was it, then, that made their fashions unique? It is important first to note that although the Hungarians were tied to the Austrian Hapsburg Empire in one way or another from 1699 until World War I, they remained culturally apart. The Austrians leaned both politically and ethnically toward the West. For centuries the Hapsburgs, through intermarriage and wars, were linked to many of the major courts of Europe. Marie-Antoinette, queen of France, and Marie-Louise, the second wife of Napoleon I, were both Austrians. The Hungarians, on the other hand, besieged by the Huns in the ninth century, occupied by the Mongols in 1241-42, and conquered by the Turks between 1541 and 1683, developed a distinct taste for oriental styles.

These differences persisted side by side during the tenure of the Austro-Hungarian Empire, creating a courtly life-style and resulting in fashions unmatched in the rest of Europe. With centuries of continuous rule behind them, the Hapsburgs had developed strong traditions growing out of medieval chivalric attitudes. The knight's armor evolved into the resplendent uniform. The romance endured, if only in fantasy. The Austrian nobleman in his courtly military regalia was grandly prepared to fight for his lady's honor. The Hungarian hussars in their spectacularly orientalized array lent further color and richness to this illusion.

Although dressed in the latest Parisian fashions, most elegant Austro-Hungarian ladies asserted a mood of ultrafemininity by their preference for light, soft fabrics in pastel colors, and added extra trimmings of laces, ruffles, and ribbons to the already excessively feminine attire in vogue at that time. They seemed as delicate as pale flower petals and appeared in sharp contrast to the strong vibrancy of their uniformed "protectors."

The Hapsburg nobility learned from Burgundian dukes of the fifteenth century to enhance its status by extending a show of opulence and a heraldic identity to male household attendants. This practice, later codified by the Spaniards into court etiquette, was limited to the most prestigious families and called for strict adherence to its rules. While the livery worn by servants was never as luxurious as the attire of their masters, it was, nevertheless, very well made, colorful, and a matter of pride to the house it represented.

World War I ended a courtly life-style that to the outside world must have had the aura of legendary romance. Neither the beautiful empress Elisabeth, nor her son, Crown Prince Rudolf, could come to terms with the aura of illusion that dominated their lives. Yet even the tragic life of the empress and the suicide of the crown prince served only to fire the imaginations of those who wanted to believe in the dream.

By the opening years of the twentieth century, the symbolism of the Hapsburg double-eagle was sadly out of step with the times. There were, however, less august but more visionary Austrians who began to prepare to meet the new era. As a part of this advance movement the famous Wiener Werkstätte was established in 1903. Here innovative artists with the help of recent technology set about to produce applied arts that would be more compatible with the new aesthetic values and changing patterns of living that the twentieth century held in promise.

Although the world of the Hapsburg dynasty no longer exists, the surviving costumes help to evoke for us some of the vanished splendor, charm, and fantasy of the Austro-Hungarian imperial era.

Stella Blum
Curator
Costume Institute

# Introduction

In the years between the two World Wars, I was often in central and eastern Europe. I felt strongly the last, long shadows cast by the empire of Austria-Hungary. All the music of the nineteenth century seemed to surround us. Roses and pleasure and dancing were everywhere.

It was then that I fell in love with the divine full-length portrait of the empress Elisabeth with her magnificent hair filled with diamond stars, which is out of the Hofburg for the first time in its history and with us here. I rarely believe anything I see in a painting, but I make an exception for Winterhalter's portrait of Elisabeth. He shows her as she was, a fantasy, a dream. Fantasy queen of a fantasy world, dream empress of a century in flight from itself.

The empire of Austria-Hungary as we are showing it to you is a sumptuous array of nineteenth-century aristocratic elegance—the court clothes, the liveries, the equipage, the military uniforms, the whiteness of the gloves, the polish of the boots, the gleaming hilts and tips of the swords. Here is Vienna, a graceful city in a graceful time, its streets and avenues filled with stately carriages and the glory of the animal; the lovely women in pale clothes, so fond of fresh flowers, strolling through the delightful parks of Schönbrunn; the gallant men with their splendid dragoon helmets shining in the sun and bright green aigrettes blowing in the wind. Here too is the land of the Magyar and its romantic capital city on the Danube, Budapest. The generous Hungarians loved their horses and vast country estates and castles; they dressed and lived entirely in their own particular splendor, quite unlike anything else in the whole of Europe with a strong hint of the Orient.

Beneath the ostentation of the scarlet and the gold, of the gilt and the brass, beneath the clatter of swords and hoofbeats, there was something more touching, more poignant. It was the rule of the emperor that no nobleman could appear at court except dressed in uniform. They were prepared to do battle with every enemy except that which would vanquish them—time. This is the empire that would also produce Klimt and Schnitzler and Freud—which would in reaction inspire and sustain the Wiener Werkstätte and the Secessionist movement—which would usher in the modern world and the twentieth century.

Diana Vreeland
Special Consultant
Costume Institute

# Austria-Hungary

━━ Frontiers of the Hapsburg Empire, 1918

▢ Kingdom of Hungary

GERMAN EMPIRE

SAXONY

Teplitz
Eger
ELBE R.
Prague
BOHEMIA
Pilsen

SILESIA
Cracow
Teschen
VISTULA R.
Premyzl
Lemberg
Tarnopol

Brünn
MORAVIA

GALICIA

BAVARIA
DANUBE R.
Straubing
Passau
Budweiss
LOWER
DANUBE R.
Vienna
Pozsony (Pressburg)

Kassa

BUKOVINA

Munich
UPPER
AUSTRIA Linz
AUSTRIA
L. FERTO
Györ
Budapest
Gödöllö
Miskolcz
TISZA R.
Debreczen
Nagyvárad

Tegernsee
Salzburg
Ischl
Innsbruck
Graz
SYRIA

VORARLBERG

KINGDOM
OF
HUNGARY

L. BALATON

TRANSYLVANIA
Kolozsvár

SWITZERLAND
Brixen
TIROL
Trent
CARINTHIA
Villach
Klagenfurt
Laibach
DRAVE R.
GORIZIA-
GRADISCA
Görz
CARNIOLA
Trieste
Zagreb

Szeged
Arad
Temesvár
MAROS R.

Venice
Milan
PO R.
ISTRIA
Fiume
Pola
CROATIA
SAVE R.
SLAVONIA

Orsova
Belgrade
ROMANIA

ITALY

ADRIATIC SEA

Zara
DALMATIA
Spalato
BOSNIA

Sarajevo

HERZO-
GOVINA
SANJAK
OF
NOVIBAZAR
MONTENEGRO
Ragusa
ALBANIA

SERBIA

DANUBE R.

BULGARIA

# Chronology

| Date | Political Events in Austria-Hungary | Political Events Elsewhere | Cultural Events |
|------|-------------------------------------|----------------------------|-----------------|
| 1699 | Turks lose Hungary and Transylvania to Austria under the terms of the Treaty of Karlowitz. Austria-Hungary becomes a major world power. | | Jean Racine (French playwright) dies. Jean-Baptiste-Siméon Chardin (French painter) is born. |
| 1700 | Charles II, king of Spain (ruled since 1665) dies, ending the Hapsburg line in Spain. Crown is inherited by Philip V, grandson of Louis XIV, who rules until 1746. | | |
| 1703 | | Peter I founds St. Petersburg. | François Boucher (French painter) is born. Construction is begun on Buckingham Palace in London. Bank of the city of Vienna is founded. |
| 1704 | Prince Eugene of Savoy and the Duke of Marlborough besiege French and Bavarian troops in Bavaria, which is occupied by Austria. England supports the Austrian archduke Karl as Spanish king in Barcelona; Philip V rules in Castile. | | |
| 1705 | Leopold I, Holy Roman Emperor since 1658, dies. He is succeeded by Joseph I, Holy Roman Emperor until 1711. | | Edmund Halley predicts the return of the comet eventually named after him for precisely 1758. (It returns early in 1759.) |
| 1711 | Joseph I dies. He is succeeded by Karl VI, Holy Roman Emperor until 1740. | England withdraws from the War of the Spanish Succession. | Leibniz meets Peter I of Russia. David Hume (English philosopher of the Enlightenment) is born. |
| 1712 | | Friedrich II (the Great) of Prussia is born. | George Frideric Handel arrives in London. |

| Date | Political Events in Austria-Hungary | Political Events Elsewhere | Cultural Events |
|------|--------------------------------------|-----------------------------|------------------|
| 1713 | The Peace of Utrecht ends the War of the Spanish Succession. Karl VI formulates his "Pragmatic Sanction," to insure the indivisibility of the Hapsburg possessions and the possibility of female succession to his throne. | | |
| 1714 | Austria declares war with Turkey. | Queen Anne of England, the last of the Stuarts, dies. She is succeeded by George II of Hanover, who is king of England until 1727. | |
| 1715 | | Louis XIV of France ("Le roi soleil") dies. He is succeeded by Louis XV, who reigns until 1747. | |
| 1717 | Maria Theresa, daughter and heir of Karl VI, is born. | | Jean-Antoine Watteau paints *Embarkation from Cythera*. |
| 1718 | Austria wins Turkish war. | | Voltaire writes *Oedipus*. Viennese porcelain manufactury is founded. |
| 1725 | | Peter I of Russia dies. | Giovanni Giacomo Casanova is born. |
| 1729 | | Catherine the Great, princess of Anhalt-Zerbst and czarina of Russia, 1762–96, is born. | Johann Sebastian Bach writes the *St. Matthew Passion*. |
| 1732 | | George Washington is born. | Franz Josef Haydn (Austrian composer) is born. Honoré Fragonard (French painter) is born. |
| 1733 | War of the Polish Succession begins; it lasts until 1738. | | François Couperin (French composer) dies. |
| 1736 | Prince Eugene of Savoy dies; Maria Theresa marries Franz Stephan of Lorraine (Franz I). | | |
| 1739 | End of the war, begun in 1735, of Austria and Russia against Turkey. | | |
| 1740 | Karl VI, Holy Roman Emperor since 1711 and king of Hungary, dies. He is succeeded by Maria Theresa, queen of Hungary and archduchess of Austria, who rules until 1780. | Karl VII of Bavaria is Holy Roman Emperor until 1745.<br><br>Friedrich Wilhelm, king of Prussia, dies. He is succeeded by Friedrich II (the Great). | French dancer Maria Anna de Camargo introduces the short ballet skirt. |
| 1742 | Maria Theresa defends Bohemia against seizure by the Prussians. | England wins French possessions in North America and India. | Handel writes his *Messiah*. |

| Date | Political Events in Austria-Hungary | Political Events Elsewhere | Cultural Events |
|---|---|---|---|
| 1745 | | Prussia recognizes Emperor Franz I as Holy Roman Emperor. Prussia receives Dresden and all of Silesia from Austria. | |
| 1748 | Austria wins the War of the Austrian Succession with Russian help. | | Jacques-Louis David (French painter) is born. Climax of the Rococo period in furniture and porcelain design. |
| 1755 | Marie Antoinette, daughter of Maria Theresa, is born. | | |
| 1756 | | Friedrich II of Prussia begins the Seven Years War against Austria. | Wolfgang Amadeus Mozart (Austrian composer) is born. |
| 1760 | | George II, king of England since 1725, dies. He is succeeded by George III, who reigns until 1820. England conquers Canada. | |
| 1765 | Franz I, husband of Maria Theresa and Holy Roman Emperor since 1745, dies. Their son Joseph II is crowned Holy Roman Emperor, which he remains until 1790. | | |
| 1770 | | Louis XVI marries Marie Antoinette. Capt. James Cook claims Australia for England. | Ludwig van Beethoven (German composer) is born. |
| 1776 | | The Declaration of Independence is signed. | The Burgtheater, one of the first German-language theaters, is founded in Vienna. |
| 1780 | Maria Theresa dies. She is succeeded by her son Joseph II, who reigns until 1790. | | Bernardo Bellotto (Canaletto; Venetian painter) dies. Jean-Auguste-Dominique Ingres (French painter) is born. |
| 1789 | | The French Revolution begins. George Washington is elected the first president of the United States. | |
| 1790 | Emperor Joseph II dies. He is succeeded by his brother Leopold II, Holy Roman Emperor until 1792. | Benjamin Franklin dies. | Mozart writes *Così fan tutte*. |
| 1792 | Leopold II dies. Franz II, a grandson of Maria Theresa, succeeds him. | France declares war on Austria. | Sir Joshua Reynolds (English painter) dies. Giacomo Rossini (Italian composer) is born. The dollar becomes the currency of the United States. |
| 1797 | | | Franz Schubert (Austrian composer) is born. |

| Date | Political Events in Austria-Hungary | Political Events Elsewhere | Cultural Events |
|------|-------------------------------------|----------------------------|-----------------|
| 1863 | England, France, and Spain place Austrian archduke Maximilian on Mexican throne. | | Theodor Billroth (Austrian physician) writes *Die allgemeine chirugische Pathologie und Therapie.* |
| 1865 | | The American Civil War ends. Gladstone becomes the leader of the Liberal party in England. | Slavery is abolished in the United States. |
| 1866 | | Otto von Bismarck starts the Prussian war against Austria. | |
| 1867 | Franz Joseph I is crowned king of Hungary. The Austro-Hungarian double monarchy lasts until 1916. Count Gyula Andrássy becomes Hungarian prime minister. | Maximilian of Mexico is executed; Mexico is again a republic. | Johann Strauss writes *The Blue Danube* waltz. Karl Marx writes *Das Kapital.* |
| 1873 | | | Viennese World Exhibition is held. Leo Tolstoy writes *Anna Karenina.* Anton Bruckner writes his Third Symphony. |
| 1889 | Archduke Rudolf and his mistress commit double suicide at Mayerling. | Adolf Hitler is born. | Auguste Rodin casts *The Thinker.* Paris World Exhibition is held. |
| 1898 | Empress Elisabeth of Austria is assassinated in Geneva. | Otto von Bismarck, Prussian statesman, dies. | |
| 1899 | | | Karl Kraus founds and writes for the liberal newspaper *Die Fackel.* Arthur Schnitzler writes *Der Reigen.* Johann Strauss dies. |
| 1914 | Archduke Franz Ferdinand and his wife, Sophie, are assassinated at Sarajevo. Austria-Hungary declares war on Serbia. World War I begins. | | Arnold Schönberg writes *Pierrot lunaire.* Walter Gropius designs headquarters for Faguswerk, a landmark of modern industrial architecture. Oskar Kokoschka paints *Tre Croix.* |
| 1916 | Franz Joseph I dies. Karl I ascends the throne of Austria-Hungary. | | Franz Kafka writes *Metamorphosis.* |
| 1918 | World War I ends. Karl I flees to Switzerland. Austria becomes a republic. Hungary is independent. | | |

*Emperor Karl I, the last Hapsburg sovereign. Oil on canvas, 1917, by Wilhelm Victor Krausz. Kunsthistorisches Museum, Vienna. Inv. no. 7287.*

# The Glory of Vienna

By Joseph Wechsberg

The glory of Austria was always very much the glory of Vienna. In this respect—only in this—Vienna always resembled Paris: it was the true capital of its country. It is often forgotten that over half a century ago Austria, Hungary, and Bohemia were the core of the Hapsburg Empire, which lasted for over six hundred years and stretched from the woods of czarist Russia to the shores of the Adriatic. In this enormous empire, where the sun almost never set, there lived a dozen nationalities with over fifty-one million people who spoke over sixteen different languages. Quite a few people spoke half a dozen languages because they had to, but no one I remember spoke all the languages of Austria-Hungary. Not surprisingly, it was the problem of nationalities and languages that eventually broke up the Hapsburg Empire.

But Vienna always remained preeminent. Not because the emperor had his residence there. For two thousand years Vienna was a gateway between West and East, a river site that had been inhabited since prehistoric times. Vienna is much older than most people realize. The oldest known relic, a small figure of a woman, known as "Venus of Willendorf," was found northwest of Vienna. It is believed to date from the Old Stone Age, from about 20,000 B.C.

Even before the Christian era there was the Celtic settlement of Vindobona. The Roman legions arrived from the south during the first century B.C. They founded the settlement of Carnuntum, in Pannonia, which no visitor to Vienna should miss seeing. In the second century A.D. Carnuntum must have been quite a place. It had an amphitheater with thirteen thousand seats. It was also the residence of the Roman emperors, whose empire then stretched from Egypt to Britannia. (Mind you, that was a thousand years before the Hapsburgs came to power in 1282.)

Vindobona was not terribly important to the Romans. They made it the garrison of the Thirteenth Legion, which was later replaced by an elite outfit, the Tenth Legion. Vindobona is a Celtic, not a Roman name, as is often assumed. In Celtic *vindo* is "white" and *bona* is "field." The emperors liked the hot springs of nearby Baden. Later Baden became known as the place where Beethoven wrote his Ninth Symphony. Later still, after the Second World War, Baden was known as the headquarters of the Soviet occupation forces. Today it is mostly known for its gambling casino. In and around Vienna history must always be considered in layers. History is very complex here and still very present.

"Vindobona" appears in old records until the end of the fifth century. By that time Christianity had spread, and the Romans, who had built roads, transplanted vines, and established Roman law, had been overrun. They couldn't fight all the tribes that beset them: the Vandals, the Marcomanni, the Visigoths, the Huns (under Attila). In A.D. 487 the last Romans were ordered home. Then came more tribes — the Langobards, the Avars, the Teutons, the Slavs, the Franks, the Bajuvars, the Magyars. All were intruders, and all left behind something of themselves: customs and costumes, traditions and folk songs, symbols and melodies. A little history is a good thing to remember. Vienna today is really the quintessence of its past.

The name "Wiennis" (Wien) appears for the first time in the Niederaltaich Annals of 1030. No one has been able to explain what happened in the preceding five hundred years. Only legends, and a few Roman and Romanesque landmarks, remain to mark the sixth through eleventh centuries. The *civitas* of Vienna came into being in 1137, shortly before the Babenbergs' arrival. Originally most Viennese were German-Austrians, but that changed when Czechs, Poles, Hungarians, and Italians appeared. The last of the Babenbergs, Duke Friedrich II, died in 1246 in the struggle against King Béla IV of Hungary. Then came the terrible interregnum when King Premysl Ottokar II of Bohemia (Fig. 2) occupied Vienna. He made himself popular by giving extravagant festivities. Even in those days the Viennese liked music and celebrations. The city became known as a place for good living. Many nobles "stayed much longer than their affairs demanded." Same as today. The most interesting thing about Vienna is that nothing has ever changed there.

In 1278 King Ottokar lost land and life on the Marchfeld, north of Vienna, to an impoverished nobleman

from the Hapsburg castle in Aargau, Switzerland. During the fourteenth century Vienna was the center of incredible calamities. In 1327 a large part of the city burned down; in 1348 there was an earthquake (for which the Jews were blamed, naturally); and a year later cholera killed tens of thousands of people.

No matter. As soon as the disaster was over, the survivors made merry. They even had Duke Otto the Merry. Dishonest bakers were put in a cage that was lowered into the Danube "amidst widespread hilarity." And all the while Austria grew, through marriages. King Matthias Corvinus of Hungary said it nicely: *Bella gerant alii; tu, felix Austria — nube!* ("Let others wage war; you, lucky Austria, marry!") By the end of the sixteenth century lucky Austria also owned Burgundy, Flanders, Germany, Hungary, and Bohemia. The Hapsburg family was an incredible success; one branch ruled in Spain and one in Vienna.

Later times in Vienna are better known. There were religious wars between Catholics and Protestants, and there was Vienna's finest hour, when a small garrison broke the second Turkish Siege, of 1683, and by common agreement of the historians saved Western civilization — for a time at least. By the mid-seventeenth century Vienna had gone through its Romanesque and Gothic periods. The evidence is still there in the first district, the inner city. The finest building of all is St. Stephen's Cathedral (Fig. 9), which was begun in 1147 and is still being built. The present cathedral is, in fact, the third structure on the site, and small parts of it are always being fixed up and renewed. St. Stephen's, beloved by the Viennese, though many don't bother to go there, shows architecturally the successive development of the Romanesque, Gothic, and Baroque styles. Churches are very important in Vienna. The bodies of the Hapsburgs were buried in the Kapuzinerkirche, their entrails were conserved in St. Stephen's Cathedral, and their hearts were kept in the Augustinerkirche.

It all sounds baroque — extravagant, bizarre, flamboyant — but Vienna remains a baroque city. "Vienna reached its cultural zenith during the Baroque, and remained baroque in its strangest and finest expressions of life," wrote Egon Friedell, who was himself a baroque mixture of essayist, philosopher, cultural historian, and actor. In Vienna the Baroque became a state of mind. Every Viennese is something of an actor who performs his part. "The whole world is a huge theater in Vienna," wrote Johann Mattheson, a critic from Hamburg, in 1728. Life has always remained a great joke for the Viennese, who have no use for the Prussians' sobriety. During the First World War it was often said in Berlin that the situation was serious but not desperate. In Vienna it was often desperate but never serious. In his verse play *Paracelsus* Arthur Schnitzler, chronicler and analyst of a glittering, decadent epoch in Vienna, wrote: "We all act parts and wise is he who knows it."

It is impossible to understand Vienna unless one understands the Viennese. They are basically a blend of people, of all the tribes and races who passed through. Whenever somebody became prominent in Prague or Cracow, in Budapest or Trieste, he would immigrate to Vienna. There were whole districts around 1900 where the people spoke only Czech, had Czech schools and Czech churches.

Vienna is known as the city of music, but of all great composers who lived there only two were Viennese, *genuine* Viennese, who were born in one district and died in another: Franz Schubert and Johann Strauss. All the other so-called Viennese composers came from elsewhere. Haydn from the Burgenland, where the Hungarian influence is very strong. Mozart from Salzburg, where the family had moved from Augsburg, in Germany. Beethoven (Fig. 6) came from Bonn, Brahms from Hamburg, Bruckner from Upper Austria, Hugo Wolf from Windischgrätz, now in Yugoslavia. Mahler from Bohemia-Moravia, Richard Strauss, once codirector of the State Opera, from Munich. But the strange, inexplicable fact is that all came to Vienna and stayed there because the *genius loci* inspired them to create.

The *genius loci* has been poetically expressed in music — all emotions in Vienna are expressed in music — by Johann Strauss (Fig. 4) in *The Blue Danube* waltz and his *Tales from the Vienna Woods* waltz. They are not his finest waltzes — I love the incredibly beautiful

*Emperor Waltz* best — but they are the musical essence of Vienna and the reason that of all great composers who lived in Vienna, Johann Strauss remains the most famous locally. The people made him their waltz king. They would have made him the waltz emperor, but they already had Emperor Franz Joseph I, whom they adored, and choosing another would have shown a lack of deference. American visitors often ask me why Johann Strauss has a beautiful monument at the Stadtpark, while the most influential Viennese in our century, Sigmund Freud, has no monument at all. Not even a street is named after him, and many streets in Vienna are named after obscure, long-forgotten people.

The explanation is simple. Strauss made the Viennese forget. "You live only once," he said. His motto is from his masterpiece, *Die Fledermaus*: "Happy is he who forgets what cannot be changed." That has always been the motto of the Viennese. They like to forget — the past, today's problems, and certainly the future. Strauss helped them forget, though he couldn't always help himself; he was often depressed and melancholy. Sigmund Freud was the antithesis. He made people remember. Who in Vienna wants to remember? And so psychoanalysis is almost unknown in the city where it was created. It took some doing from abroad, as late as 1971, to turn Freud's apartment, where he had lived for over fifty years and had created his most important works, into a modest museum.

The Viennese are very paradoxical people. They didn't like their greatest composers. Emperor Joseph II once asked the second-rate composer Dittersdorf whether Haydn wasn't "dallying" too much. Haydn, a great genius, was never popular in Vienna. Neither was Mozart (Fig. 6). *Le Nozze di Figaro* was soon forgotten, while *Cosa Rara* by Vicente Martin y Solar, a now mercifully forgotten Italianized Spaniard, was received with enthusiasm. When Rossini came to Vienna in 1822, after the deserved success of *Il Barbiere di Siviglia*, the much greater local composers Beethoven and Schubert were ignored. Beethoven was totally misunderstood. His only local success was his symphony *Wellington's Victory*, with realistic battlefield sounds, which he himself later called "nonsense." Apparently in

THE IMPERIAL STYLE

*Fig. 5. Franz Schubert and his friends. Watercolor, 1821, by Leopold Kupelwieser. Austrian National Library. Photo: The Bettmann Archive.*

*Fig. 6. Beethoven appearing before Mozart and the Viennese elite. Detail of a wood engraving, mid-nineteenth century. Photo: The Bettmann Archive.*

Vienna genius was understood only by a fellow genius. Haydn was the only one who praised *Don Giovanni,* and Mozart in turn admired Haydn. Mozart said of Beethoven, then seventeen years old: "Someday the world will notice him." Schubert was too shy to speak when he saw Beethoven in the street, but he confided to his diary: "Who would dare to attempt *anything* after Beethoven?" And Beethoven, who read some Schubert songs on his deathbed, is reported to have said, "Truly, he has the divine spark."

One could go on and on. Gustav Mahler, admired as director and chief conductor at the Court Opera, where even today people speak of his magnificent productions of the works of Mozart and Wagner, was booed across the Ringstrasse when his new symphonies were performed at the Musikverein. A complete cycle of his works was not given in Vienna until the 1960s, long after they had conquered America. The three heroes of what is now called modern music — Arnold Schönberg, Alban Berg, and Anton von Webern — met with hostility from Viennese audiences. Yet the fact remains that this incredible city is now considered the cradle of three great musical schools: classicism, romanticism, and modern music. No other city on earth can make a similar claim — except perhaps Athens at the time of Pericles or the Florence of the Medicis.

Schubert (Fig. 5) was long portrayed by his biographers as a happy-go-lucky bohemian, the composer of Merry Old Vienna. That was the silly image created by the operetta legend of *Blossom Time,* and perhaps too by the inaccurate memories of his friends. Only now, a hundred and fifty years after his death, is the true story of Schubert known: struggling, ill, and often in debt, he was completely ignored outside the small circle of his friends. But his music has always told the truth; there is often a haunting melancholy in the works of Schubert, just as there is in the music of Johann Strauss. Both were basically melancholy people. So are many Viennese, all of whom have a reputation for constantly laughing, always ready for another waltz (Fig. 3).

Strangely, they are. Vienna's *Fasching* (carnival) has to be seen to be believed. It begins unofficially on New Year's Eve, when the State Opera puts on a gala per-formance of *Die Fledermaus.* The prices of tickets are the highest on earth, but the event is always sold out. At the same time the Vienna Philharmonic, Vienna's most prestigious orchestra, which also furnishes musicians for the orchestra of the Opera House, plays the waltzes and polkas of the members of the Strauss dynasty and of Josef Lanner, the erstwhile friend of the older Strauss. This pleasant custom was started by the late Clemens Krauss, a born-and-bred Viennese who understood the musical soul of Vienna. For the past twenty-five years Willi Boskovsky, the Philharmonic's former concertmaster, has conducted the concerts, which are repeated on New Year's Day, with dances executed by the ballet of the State Opera. The event is televised all over the world. The waltzes of Strauss are beloved in the East and in the West. Even the elaborate showmanship cannot kill the spirit, and people all over the world sigh at the thought of this imperishable, charming city. Boskovsky's successor is Lorin Maazel.

Between New Year's Day and Ash Wednesday there are literally thousands of balls (Fig. 8) in Vienna. Balls for Vienna's society (the Philharmoniker-Ball), for millionaires and general managers from abroad (the Opernball, where boxes go for fifty thousand schillings, some four thousand dollars, and yet are always sold out), and balls for members of the police, for the firemen, for the pastry makers, and so on. Every ball is crowded. A common question is, "Where and when do the Viennese sleep during *Fasching?*" The answer is, "At the place where they work, where else?" Yet it would be wrong to deduce that the Viennese are lazy. They are simply *Lebenskünstler* — gifted at having great fun at low rates. It is also true that they always spend a little more than they should. Yet the people of Vienna nicely manage to crowd work and entertainment into their schedules.

The Austrians refer to their country as an *Insel der Seligen* — island of the blessed. They are on good terms with eastern and western countries; a while ago the president of the German Federal Republic came to dance at the Opernball, and then the Austrian president went to neighboring Czechoslovakia, where they showed him factories and state farms. As King Matthias

28

Fig. 9. St. Stephen's
Cathedral. Engraving, by
Ladislaus Rupp, from
Pianta Elevazione, e
Spaccato della Ciesa di San
Stefano, di Vienna,
published in 1794. The
Metropolitan Museum of
Art, New York. Rogers
Fund, 1952. 52.519.167b.

Corvinus said, "Let others wage war." Austria declared itself neutral when the Soviets moved out in 1955; to this day no one can tell why they left. The Austrian currency is stable, much more so than the once almighty dollar, and Vienna has become one of the most expensive cities on earth.

The Viennese know a great deal about music, but little about the second most important creative art. Every building with no distinct architectural style is called "baroque." Local architects even invented their own style, called "Viennese," or "Ringstrasse." The term was coined in 1857, when Emperor Franz Joseph I decided to make Vienna a truly imperial city by surrounding old Vienna, the first district, with a *via triumphalis* — the Ringstrasse — that would be the visible symbol of his empire. He had no illusions even then; he knew that the empire was falling apart.

During the second half of the nineteenth century, when Austria went through a series of military, political, and economic disasters, the imperial city was created, at great expense. There was already a wealth of architectural beauty, the fine Church of St. Rupert, Vienna's oldest, in pure Romanesque style, and the purely Gothic St. Maria am Gestade, once the church of the fishermen. There was St. Stephen's Cathedral, landmark and symbol of the city. There were the masterpieces of the Viennese baroque, different from the original, Italian Baroque and the baroque in Prague and Dresden. During the seventeenth century Vienna had become a city of palaces. The rich noblemen became dilettante architects and amateur builders. (That was before the Liechtensteins, the Schönborns, the Schwarzenbergs, and Starhembergs discovered the great composers and became patrons of their art.)

Vienna had the two greatest baroque architects: Johann Bernhard Fischer von Erlach and Lucas von Hildebrandt. Fischer's masterpiece is the Karlskirche — bizarre and beautiful, flanked by two "Trajanesque" columns (Fig. 11). It is sometimes called a "theatrical" church, but that doesn't seem to bother the Viennese. Fischer died in 1723, before the church was completed. Hildebrandt's masterpiece was built for Austria's "secret emperor," Prince Eugene of Savoy, the greatest

military man of his time, who decisively defeated the Turks and expanded the empire of Karl VI. He never bothered to learn German and signed his name "Eugenio von Savoye." He already had a winter palace on Himmelpfortgasse (for the past hundred fifty years it has been Austria's ministry of finance), and he commissioned Hildebrandt to build his summer palace on the finest site in Vienna, a slope overlooking the city, with the silhouette of Kahlenberg in the background. (Canaletto's nephew, Bernardo Bellotto, who was also called Canaletto in Vienna, painted the beautiful view.) At the foot of the slope Hildebrandt built the Lower Belvedere, which the Viennese pronounce in the French manner — "Belvedèr-e." From there a terraced formal garden leads to the Upper Belvedere, where the secret emperor gave his great receptions and talked with his famous friends, among them Leibniz, Voltaire, and Rousseau. Assuming the emperor's prerogative, the little prince kept his hat on when he received foreign dignitaries.

From the Belvedere Archduke Franz Ferdinand and his wife, whom he loved so much that he married her against the wish of the emperor, went to Sarajevo, their last journey (Fig. 10). On May 15, 1955, the State Treaty was signed in the Upper Belvedere by Dulles, Macmillan, Molotov, Pinay, and Leopold Figl, Austria's late foreign minister, and once more Austria belonged to the Austrians. Today paintings and sculptures are exhibited in the Belvedere. Everybody knows that the world's finest Pieter Brueghel collection is at the Kunsthistorisches Museum, but not everybody bothers to go up to the Upper Belvedere. Few people know that Anton Bruckner, the one-time organist at the baroque monastery of St. Florian in Upper Austria, wrote his last symphony in the small custodian's lodge next to the glorious baroque palace and died there in 1893. His symphonies will still be heard when the Belvedere is merely a pile of rubble.

But back to the Ringstrasse, which was to be the great showcase of the emperor's vanishing power. The first great building completed was the new Court Opera, now known as the State Opera. If St. Stephen's Cathedral remains the soul of Vienna, the Opera House

Fig. 10. Archduke Franz
Ferdinand and his wife,
Countess Chotek, who
were assassinated at
Sarajevo, Yugoslavia,
August 1914. The Bett-
mann Archive.

(Fig. 7) is its beating heart. People come from every-where for performances there. On many evenings the performance may be merely routine; so are many per-formances in New York, London, Paris, Milan. But an evening at the Opera House is almost always an experi-ence. Moritz von Schwind, a friend of Franz Schu-bert, painted the lunettes of the loggias. They survived the terrible fire that broke out when the Opera House was accidentally hit by American bombers toward the end of the last war. No one in Vienna was much sur-prised when the Opera was rebuilt right away, while the people went hungry and cold; the much-needed hospitals, schools, and dwellings had to wait. The Opera was more important. What would Vienna be without its musical heart?

When the emperor had seemed displeased because the Opera House was not a tall, commanding structure like the Paris Opéra, one of the architects committed suicide and the other died two months later "of a bro-ken heart." Everybody understood. For the baroque citizens of Vienna death is always nearby. They love beautiful funerals. The composer Hugo Wolf was widely ignored while he was alive, but everybody was at his funeral. If a member of the State Opera dies, the coffin is carried twice around "the house."

After the Neo-Renaissance Opera House, the two court museums were finished along the Ring. The Kunsthistorisches Museum houses the great collec-tions formed by the Hapsburgs. The Italian collection is remarkable, with Bellinis, Giorgiones, Lottos, Palmas, Titians, and Tintorettos. The two museums are also built in Neo-Renaissance style.

Next came the Neo-Hellenistic Parliament, built by the great Danish architect Theophil Hansen; the Neo-Gothic Town Hall, built by a German, Friedrich Schmidt; and, across from it, the Neo-Renaissance Burgtheater, which the Viennese like to call "the lead-ing German-language theater in Europe." (Not every-body in Germany and Switzerland agrees.)

The neostyles or pseudostyles of the great Ring-strasse buildings were bitterly criticized by the younger generation, but it must be admitted that the great avenue, flanked by two rows of linden trees, with

Fig. 11. View of the Karls-
kirche and the municipal
hospital, Vienna. Detail of
an engraving, by Salomon
Kleiner, from Vera et
Accurata Delineatio...
Caesarea Sede Vienna,...
published by J. A. Pfeffel,
Augsburg, 1725. The
Metropolitan Museum of
Art, New York. Harris
Brisbane Dick Fund, 1930.
30.68.19 (2).

large parks and wide green spaces between the buildings, is very attractive. The Ringstrasse had its great
moment in 1879, when Emperor Franz Joseph I
and Empress Elisabeth ("Sisi") celebrated their silver
wedding anniversary with a magnificent parade-
extravaganza arranged by Hans Makart.

The reaction was bound to come. Nine years later
Adolf Loos, a brilliant architect, compared Vienna to
"Potemkin's Town." He hated the pretentious Ringstrasse style created during "an era of parvenus," with
stucco ornaments made to look like stone and marble.
By 1898 a group of young artists had already "seceded"
from the Künstlerhaus, Vienna's art establishment, and
had founded the Secession. Suddenly Vienna became a
springboard for the phenomenon of modern art.
One remembers Gustav Klimt (Fig. 12) and Oskar

Kokoschka; the gifted Egon Schiele, who died at the
age of twenty-eight; the great architect Otto Wagner;
Joseph Hoffmann and Koloman Moser, who created the
Wiener Werkstätte. In 1910 Adolf Loos, practicing what
he preached, built the first truly functional apartment
house ("the house without eyebrows") in Michaeler
Square, across from the venerable Hofburg. Looking
out of his window, the emperor could not fail to see the
elegant, austere facade that lacked even a single
ornament.

Meanwhile, the writers of Vienna had supported the
artists and architects. But the heyday of the great
playwright-actors Ferdinand Raimund and Johann
Nestroy was past. Nestroy in particular had told the
Viennese terrible things, but he had also made them
laugh, and the Viennese have always accepted amusing

criticism by a Viennese (not by outsiders). They grudgingly accepted Karl Kraus, a great moralist, and lately they have accepted the satirist Helmut Qualtinger.

The literary rebellion against bourgeois narrow-mindedness and the cultural decay of the Ringstrasse style centered around *Jung Wien* (Young Vienna) — around Hermann Bahr, Arthur Schnitzler, and Hugo von Hofmannsthal. There were other luminaries too, now remembered in Vienna but elsewhere forgotten, like the eccentric coffeehouse poet Peter Altenberg and the poet Richard Beer-Hofmann. Everybody was fighting the battles of their fellow creative artists. The writers supported Arnold Schönberg's new theories. Schönberg, an able painter, too, painted Alban Berg, who was a friend of Kokoschka. Schnitzler once said he would rather do without Goethe than without Beethoven. Schnitzler and Sigmund Freud admired each other. Many members of what was known as the Viennese medical school played instruments and had chamber music at home. Theodor Billroth, the great surgeon, to whom Brahms dedicated some works, played the piano and viola well.

One could go on and on. The writers had their own coffeehouses. Grillparzer, Lenau, Raimund, and Stifter met at Neuner's, and later the writers of Young Vienna had their tables at the Café Griensteidl. Freud, Billroth, and, later, Victor Adler and T. G. Masaryk (who became the founder and first president of Czechoslovakia) met at the Café Central. The first coffeehouse in Vienna was opened in 1684, a year after the Turkish Siege. By 1925 there were over 1,250 coffeehouses in the city. Coffeehouse life, a very Viennese way of life, ended in 1938. Whether the institution of the coffeehouse will survive is not certain. Times have changed.

What hasn't changed is the amazing heritage left by rulers, composers, poets, architects, and doctors — the seemingly indestructible institutions such as Demel's, the best known of Vienna's fifteen hundred pastry shops, and the *Heuriger* (wine taverns) in the suburbs, where the new wine is drunk. Today Vienna is no longer the capital of an empire, but of a country with less than eight million people. Almost every fourth Austrian is a Viennese. They haven't changed, and they never will; they live well on the heritage of a brilliant past.

Georg Fischenthaller Müllermeister am Alster
Bach verkauft alhier Mehl und Grik das Achtl
vor ein kreuzer Wohlfeiller als auf den Markt.

# The Beautiful Viennese:

## Fashions from the Time of Maria Theresa to the End of the Congress of Vienna

By Reingard Witzmann, Assistant to the Director, Museen der Stadt Wien

The history of fashion in Vienna reads like a "comedy of vanity"; most of what we know about Viennese fashion in the eighteenth century has come down to us in the words of contemporary moralists who raged against the frivolity and luxury of women's clothes and condemned them as immoral imitations of French styles. In fact, fashion criticism in Vienna began well before there was an established Viennese style. The decades of constant criticism had the effect of stimulating the local garment trades, and it was the resulting economic renaissance that laid the foundations for a distinctive Viennese style.

The first moves toward economic self-sufficiency had begun in the seventeenth century. In 1684 an essay by P. W. von Hörnicke called "Austria Above All, If Only It Puts Its Mind to It" was published and very favorably received. During the reigns of Maria Theresa (1740–80) and Joseph II (1780–90) Vienna became a true competitor in the international market for manufactured goods. The importation of foreign fabrics and porcelains was repeatedly prohibited to encourage local trades. The porcelain industry was nationalized by Maria Theresa and was world renowned by 1744; silk weaving was similarly sponsored. In 1763 Maria Theresa passed a patent that provided for the planting of white mulberry trees for the cultivation of silk worms. Mulberry trees had already been planted outside the gates of Vienna, in Rossau, and in the courtyards of the newly constructed hospital. The plan was for the hospital to administer the silk industry as a profitable sideline.

After 1780 the suburb of Schottenfeld became the center of the silk trade and was popularly called "Brilliantengrund" ("field of diamonds"). At the beginning of the nineteenth century more than thirty thousand workers were employed there, and the silks they produced soon enjoyed international renown. Between 1812 and 1816 almost two million pounds of silk were made into dresses. The silk dyers had been unionized since 1773. It took four or five years of apprenticeship to learn the difficult techniques of their trade. For example, the different shades of white could be obtained only by a complex process of boiling the fabric in oily soap and color additives.

*Fig. 16. Caricature on
contemporary fashions.
Detail of a hand-colored
etching, about 1785, by
Hieronymus Löschenkohl.
Museen der Stadt Wien.
Inv. no. 62.064.*

THE IMPERIAL STYLE

Fig. 17. Sketch for a
fashion plate showing day
dresses, one with a spencer.
Watercolor, about 1798.
Museen der Stadt Wien.
Inv. no. 97.741/2.

In the transition period as Rococo gave way to Classicism—between 1780 and 1820—the fashion that developed in Vienna took its flavor from the ethnic costumes worn in the many Hapsburg-ruled states. In the course of the eighteenth century the population of Vienna had grown from 80,000 to 210,000. The first influx of population can be attributed to the Turkish Siege of 1683. Afterward people flocked from the rural areas to the city. These new arrivals were not only a source of cheap labor, but also an infusion of cultural enrichment for the city. At first they retained their rural customs as well as their national costumes and were not immediately assimilated into city life. Such groups lived outside the city fortifications, in the suburbs that extended up to the old city limit (today the area between the Ringstrasse and the Gürtelstrasse). In 1790 there were 1,312 houses in the city proper, but 5,241 in the suburbs.

The social structure of the time was reflected in the dresses of the women and young girls. In many portraits of women from the time of Joseph II one sees a complete synthesis of urban fashion and ethnic costume in the clothes of chambermaids and cooks as well as bourgeois women. The idea of dressing in layers came from traditional rural costumes: over a corset, called a "little bouffant," a woman wore a short, tight jacket—a spencer—and a voluminous skirt with an apron. On her head she wore a bonnet of cloth or gold (Fig. 14). Every woman wore a variation of this ensemble. There had been no dress code since 1766, when Maria Theresa had been forced to retract one she had passed for "religious, moral, and economic" reasons. Thanks to the new freedom, any woman might dress as she wished. The only indication of class differences was the richness of the materials used; a bourgeois matron's dress was stiffer, more expensive, and less coquettish than that of a chambermaid.

The gold bonnets were popular in Vienna from the end of the eighteenth century until the time of the Congress of Vienna (1814–15). The gold cloth and embroidery, fragile tinsel, and gold sequins that went into making the bonnets were local products. The headdress was worn all along the Danube on the "gold-

Fig. 18. *A lady of fashion in an Empire-style dress and Schute. Watercolor, pen and ink, 1810, by Johann Adam Klein. Museen der Stadt Wien. Inv. no. 108.207.*

Fig. 19. *At a morning concert in the Augarten. Watercolor, pen and sepia, about 1820, by Georg Emanuel Opitz. Museen der Stadt Wien. Inv. no. S. N. 4.486.*

bonnet route," with shapes and styles varying from province to province. Because they were precious, the bonnets were highly prized and were passed down in families as heirlooms.

Ironically, the women of the very lowest class in Vienna took over the pannier skirt from the ladies of the nobility (Fig. 15). In the 1780s these developed into absurdly wide skirts called "bouffants" and were mocked in word and picture (Fig. 16). Joseph II tried to curb prostitution by forcing ladies of pleasure unlucky enough to be arrested to sweep the streets in shorn hair and excessive bouffants, therefore the popularity of these exaggerated "excrescences" lasted only a few years. And some women of the lower classes—the chambermaids, for instance—never embraced them. The social critic Johann Pezzl wrote: "At a time when the elegant ladies of the world threw themselves into the disgusting bouffants,... only the chambermaids were witty enough not to hide their pretty figures under that despicable broadness which seems like two donkeys attached to their sides."

The French Revolution of 1789 brought about an abrupt shift in the history of European fashion. Since political upheaval is always accompanied by propaganda, even dress becomes a symbol. The failure of the middle-class revolution of 1848 in Vienna is underscored by the fact that it did not affect the way people dressed. On the other hand, the French Revolution had transformed the Rococo style into one of "republican simplicity" in Paris. This desire for simplicity was very much behind the revival of antique forms at the end of the eighteenth century. The high-waisted dress of the Hellenistic era allowed the body to be nearly visible through the garment. This "chemise greque" made its first appearance in the almanacs of 1789–90. It was a shirtlike dress without sleeves, worn with flat slippers with crossed ribbons tied at the ankles. Once this simple style took hold, high coiffures, hip pads, high heels, and laced bodices were considered confessions of counterrevolutionary sympathies.

The Empire style, which originated in Paris, was soon taken up enthusiastically by the Viennese. The ladies of Vienna had always appreciated a certain kind

THE IMPERIAL STYLE

of simplicity, which the twentieth-century writer Egon Friedell described as "a pleasing inclination toward discretion." The fashion-conscious Viennese got the latest information on the Parisian styles through the French fashion journal *Cabinet des Modes*, published in Vienna by the resourceful art dealer Hieronymus Löschenkohl.

Even though the Viennese remained influenced by clothes from Paris and London—the latter especially affected men's fashions—they never adopted a style without adding certain distinctive touches of their own. In the richly illustrated miniature fashion almanacs, which served as the only local fashion journals until 1816, one can trace the evolution of style in Vienna. In his *Calendar of Love, Tenderness Dedicated to the Fair Sex*, published in 1789, the entrepreneurial Löschenkohl stated that "the enduring applause which the public has bestowed on my fashion calendars makes it my duty to once again excerpt the most beautiful models for this year and to deliver them to you. . . . They are from the best foreign journals, from my own correspondence, and from the creative genius of our beautiful German ladies."

In the Viennese adaptation of the Empire style, the airy chemise dress was worn with a spencer, usually red (Fig. 17). The Viennese ladies preferred silk for day dresses, although some still wore the very sheer fabrics that had led to pneumonia—appropriately called "mousseline illness." As headgear, the ladies often wore a helmetlike hat, from which the bonnet (*Schute*) later developed (Fig. 18). White was the predominant fashion color; it was used for day and evening wear, and if a fabric was enlivened with woven or embroidered motifs, the background was invariably white. "What is color compared to form?" asked Georg Foster in his *Opinions from the Lower Rhine*.

The period from 1780 to 1820 is known as "Viennese classic" in music and fashion. The same classicizing spirit that is evident in Haydn's compositions can be seen in the lines of contemporary clothing. At the same time, an undercurrent of the "folk" influence can also be discerned. Many visitors to Vienna tried to describe its attractions. Johann Friedrich Reichert wrote in

1808: "For the whole morning the Augarten [one of Vienna's most attractive parks] was a true garden of delights filled with a beautiful, refined world, and I have never seen a more beautiful combination of lovely skin, delicate, voluptuous flesh, and magnificent robes. The midday terrace of the Tuileries in Paris seems like a colorful field of tulips compared to this enchanting meadow of hyacinths" (Fig. 19).

The Congress of Vienna brought about a period of calm after the ongoing wars with Napoleon, who had occupied Vienna in 1809 and had even blown up a small part of the city's fortifications. On December 26, 1815, the emperor of Austria, the king of Prussia, and the czar of Russia signed a three-way treaty that was later undersigned by almost all the other European nations. The pact, known as the "Holy Alliance," was aimed at achieving world peace through strict maintenance of the political status quo. As a result, the political policy of Austria after 1815 became one of opposition to all revolutionary movements. Statesman Klemens von Metternich's stringent antipolitical doctrine called for more government involvement in private affairs. This brought a new insularity to Viennese daily life and a new emphasis on the family and the arts. The people's desire for joie de vivre now found expression "indoors." Chamber music enjoyed a new vogue, as did dances held at home. The courtly minuet gave way to the exuberant waltz.

Industrial technology kept pace with the increased tempo of social life. The enormous quantity of raw materials and the improving methods of manufacture made the rapidly changing fashions available to an ever greater number of the people. In 1816 Vienna had a population of more than 250,000. There were more than 1,272 middle-class tailors in the city (and 388 "competent" tailors were operating without licenses). After the Congress of Vienna there was even a surplus of clothes, so that by 1820 the importation of new and used clothing "with or without fur linings" was strictly prohibited by law.

After the biweekly *Wiener Modenzeitung* began publication in 1816, it became the voice of the Viennese couturiers. Artists like the painter Johann Ender

THE IMPERIAL STYLE

*Fig. 20. Dance dress.*
*Colored copper engraving,*
*1818, by Johann Blaschke*
*after Johann Ender,*
*published in* Wiener
Zeitschrift für Kunst,
Literatur und Mode, *vol.*
*7, no.3. Museen der Stadt*
*Wien. Inv. no. 56.740/38.*

(1793–1854) and Philipp von Stubenrauch (1784–1848), director of the costume workshops of the imperial theaters, illustrated the original designs of the Viennese designers, which were often produced as hand-colored fashion plates. The magazine was renamed the *Wiener Zeitschrift für Kunst, Literatur und Mode* when it changed its editorial scope and became a general-interest publication.

The many dances given by the middle class in their own dance halls hastened the development of a dance dress that expressed the naturalness and simplicity of the age. The dress that evolved was made in two pieces: an underdress of satin and an overdress of cotton or the thinnest silk, which allowed the dancer freedom of movement even as she executed the most complicated steps (Fig. 20).

The dynamic waltzes of Josef Lanner and Johann Strauss the Elder gave wings to their audiences and swept them up in a happy dream. The Biedermeier style was to be the complete expression of that sweet and harmonious time that ended abruptly with the middle-class revolution of 1848.

Fig. 21. The Congress of Vienna. Franz I is at center; Wellington, with raised scroll, is behind the globe, right; Talleyrand is at far right. Engraving, 1814, by I. Zurz. The Metropolitan Museum of Art, New York. Gift of Miss Georgiana W. Sargent in memory of John Osborne Sargent, 1924. 24.63.2009.

# Viennese Biedermeier Fashion

By Helga Kessler, Lewisohn Fellow, The Costume Institute, The Metropolitan Museum of Art

The term "Biedermeier" originated with a series of poetic parodies published in the satirical magazine *Fliegende Blätter* between 1855 and 1857 by two German writers, L. Eichrodt and A. Kussmaul. The series, titled "Poems of the Swabian Schoolmaster Gottlieb Biedermaier,..." made use of the fictitious character "Herr Biedermaier" to poke fun at a class of staunch conservatives whose ideal it was to live unobtrusively, self-contentedly, and comfortably within its own four walls. (*Bieder* in German means "upright, staunch, loyal, trustworthy"; "Maier" or "Meier" is a common surname.) It was only toward the end of the nineteenth century that this term was used by historians to describe the earlier years of the century, and "Biedermeier" soon became synonymous with "the good old days." The name is now applied to the years from 1815 to 1848—from the end of the Napoleonic Wars to the revolution of 1848.

"Biedermeier" has come to stand for a life-style that expressed itself in the arts, philosophy, and fashions. The Viennese Biedermeier developed its own particular flavor and can perhaps be considered the most typical version of the Biedermeier style, although the Biedermeier also pervaded western Europe as well as America.

The Congress of Vienna is considered the starting point of this era. This event, which lasted nearly a whole year, from 1814 to 1815, put Vienna on the map politically as well as socially in the eyes of Europe. Statesmen and military heroes like Wellington from England, Talleyrand from France, and the powerful monarchs of the European nations—the czar of Russia, the king of Prussia, and many princes of the smaller states—came together in Vienna to decide the fate of the European nations left in upheaval after the defeat of Napoleon (Fig. 21). It was Klemens von Metternich, the brilliant and flamboyant Austrian statesman, who dominated the proceedings. Metternich's great political aims were ultimately not realized, but his "Holy Alliance," a peace treaty among Russia, Prussia, and Austria, was signed. This ultraconservative, monarchist, and Christian (Catholic) policy became the fundament of the so-called System Metternich, which determined Austria's political position until 1848. The congress, of which the witty Count de la Gardé wrote, *Le congrès il ne marche pas—il danse*, was the social event of the century. Never had so many crowned heads gathered in one place. The beautiful women of the courts of all Europe were part of the entourages of the rulers and naturally participated in the ceaseless festivities that punctuated the year of the congress. The beauties of the Viennese aristocracy—Countess Wrbna Auersperg, the Hungarian Countess Zichy-Festeticz, and the French-born Countess Eszterházy-Roisin, and many more shone in the brilliance of the endless soirees, balls, corsos, and masked balls.

For Vienna, and particularly for the Viennese fashion industry, the congress was the catalyst in the development of a distinctive Viennese style. The Viennese tailors were suddenly required to produce uniforms for the visiting dignitaries, who were most demanding as to cut and fit. This training in perfection prepared the tailors who were to produce the brilliant fashions of the future in Vienna. The ladies of Vienna and everywhere in Europe ordered their grand toilettes from Paris during the days of the congress, but they commissioned their lesser gowns from the Viennese couturiers. Bertuch, a journalist writing for the *Journal des Luxus und der Mode*, published in Weimar, wrote from Vienna shortly before the congress that the Viennese ladies did not want to set the tone in fashion, but preferred instead to let the international spectacle pass before them. This attitude changed significantly after the congress. In 1816 the *Wiener Modenzeitung*, the first Viennese fashion journal, appeared. Paris and London had long had their own fashion journals, but Vienna had lagged behind until now. The magazine, which included articles on art, literature, music, science, and travel, was written for the social and intellectual elite and is a wonderful document of the Biedermeier era, since it did not cease publication until 1848, the end of the period. The fashion plates, drawn by the artist Johann Ender after creations of the Viennese couturiers Beer, Petko, and Bohlinger, soon became known as the most beautiful in Europe. The drawings were of high quality, and the plates were carefully etched and hand

*Fig. 23. Redingote.*
*Fashion plate forty-three*
*for 1817 in the* Wiener
Zeitschrift für Kunst,
Literatur und Mode. *The*
*Metropolitan Museum of*
*Art, New York. Thomas J.*
*Watson Library.*

*Fig. 22. Dance dress.*
*Fashion plate six for 1817*
*in the* Wiener Zeitschrift
für Kunst, Literatur und
Mode. *The Metropolitan*
*Museum of Art, New York.*
*Thomas J. Watson Library.*

THE IMPERIAL STYLE

colored. Since they are illustrations of actual clothes, they convey a very accurate picture of the Viennese Biedermeier style.

Until 1816 Vienna had been entirely dependent on the fashion trends set in Paris, but, with the defeat of Napoleon and the triumphant air the congress produced, there was a determined effort to be liberated from the French fashion dictatorship. The slender silhouette of the Empire dress, with its high waistline slightly modified, still dominated the scene. The most fashionable color was still white, and the very sheer materials like muslin and batiste remained the Viennese ladies' favorites. New, however, were the decorations of *vapeur* lace, embroidery, and openwork on the bodices and sleeves and at the hems of the skirts. The accessories—flat shoes tied with ribbons, the gloves, the trimmings of the bonnets—were all made in pastel colors. Typical of the graceful forms of the early Biedermeier were airy dance dresses. The example illustrated (Fig. 22) was made of *petinet*, a lacelike material, and decorated with petals of green satin and a ruffle of blonde lace at the décolleté. The accessories were invariably lace-trimmed gloves worn to cover the elbow, leaving a bit of bare arm between them and the short, puffed sleeve. Coquettish too was the shortness of the dress; dance dresses were much shorter than day dresses and revealed a lady's delicate satin slippers and her white stockings. The playfulness and lightheartedness of this creation seems to be the very embodiment of a ländler or a waltz by Schubert.

Although Austria was in poor financial condition in the years after the Napoleonic Wars, and stringent economy measures were necessary in almost every aspect of life, music and dance flourished in Vienna. The little dance dresses made in the years between 1816 and 1820 show that the Viennese ladies, always more conservative than their Parisian counterparts, could convert a simple style into something very elegant and charming. It was the Viennese predilection for details, lovingly executed, that gave these dresses their special quality. The ornaments—the little lace ruffles at the décolleté, at the cuffs of the sleeves, and at the hem of the skirts—gave a coordinated feeling to the dresses.

The colors remained pastels: light pinks and blues and still much white, but delicate stripes became popular, too. The change in silhouette was gradual; the waistline remained high, but the skirts began to be fuller and were gathered at the back. The thrifty Viennese even designed ball gowns with double sleeves; long sleeves could be detached from short, puffed ones so that the dress could be worn all year round. The always practical Viennese ladies ridiculed and rejected the preposterous demands of Caroline Pichler, a member of the literati and a lady-in-waiting at court, who published her theory for a strict dress code in 1818. She was very much influenced by the romantic literature of her day and was no doubt inspired by masked balls, which were often based on medieval chivalric themes and required costumes in the medieval style. Pichler seriously proposed that the empress dictate a style of dress to be worn by all ladies; this archetypal style could not be altered, although it could be produced in a variety of colors. Pichler herself was portrayed by painter Carl von Sales in a "medieval" dress of dark blue velvet with "medievally"slit sleeves, but with a high waistline like the dresses of her day. It speaks well of the Viennese ladies that they merely shrugged their shoulders and continued to wear their pretty, light dresses. Sometimes there are medieval or "alt-deutsche" details on the dresses in the plates of the *Wiener Modenzeitung,* but one never sees anything as radical as an entirely medieval-style dress. The general taste ran more to "modern" things; plaids and stripes became more and more popular not only for dresses but also for coats — the so-called redingotes. Several of those illustrated in the *Wiener Modenzeitung* show the strong influence of uniforms, which were seen in such profusion on the streets of Vienna during and after the congress. The ladies, for instance, adopted the epaulets and the Hungarian passementerie from the uniforms of the dashing hussars and applied them to their redingotes (Fig. 23). No lady was seen in public without her gloves and a hat. The bonnets of the early Biedermeier, called *Schuten* in German, had wide brims that hid the profile and were securely tied under the chin. They were made of satin or straw and trimmed under the brim and on the crown with colorful ribbons and artificial flowers. The coiffures—more elaborate for balls and soirees—were always arranged with the hair in a center part, then curled at the temples and worn in a chignon at the back of the head. Over the years great imagination was used to contrive more and more intricate and elaborate knotting and trimmings for the hair. Other accessories, such as jewelry, were sparse in the early Biedermeier, mainly because the Austrians had had to surrender their gold and silver jewelry to the government during the Napoleonic Wars. For a short time

Fig. 25. The return of
Emperor Franz I to Vienna
after the meeting of
parliament in Pressburg
(Pozsony), 1809. Oil on
canvas, 1825, by Peter
Krafft. Kunsthistorisches
Museum, Vienna. Photo:
Meyer, Vienna.

THE IMPERIAL STYLE

jewelry made of iron had been popular, but in the years following the congress the Viennese ladies managed to be dazzling even without precious metals and stones. A particularly charming accessory much used in Vienna was a little ball of silver wire worn at the wrist on a braceletlike band (Fig. 24). The ladies would carry their knitting or crocheting to parties in these balls, so as to participate in the fun, yet remain virtuously busy.

During the 1820s Austria continued to recover from the financial depression. A stable government—with Metternich as chancellor after 1821 and Franz I as the emperor who left politics to the politicians—accounted for a slow but steady increase in wealth. Industry, particularly the furniture and textile trades, began to thrive in Vienna. The architects Peter Nobile and Joseph Kornhäusel created buildings like the Theseustempel in the Volksgarten (1823) and the charming Josefstädter Theater (1826–32) as well as Neoclassical villas in Baden, a little watering spot just outside Vienna. These buildings are all much less elaborate than the Baroque and Rococo palaces of Vienna, but have a simple elegance all their own. They were furnished in what we consider the "actual Biedermeier style," in which comfort and practicality took precedence over luxury. The straight lines of the tables and chairs and the flowered upholstery and drapes created a truly bourgeois atmosphere of *Gemütlichkeit*. It was in this setting that most Viennese social life took place during the Biedermeier. Public gatherings were frowned upon, if not actually forbidden, by the strictly enforced police state of the System Metternich. But in private homes, no matter how frugally furnished, friends gathered to read aloud, listen to music, and dance. It was a period when artistic patronage was the province of the middle class. The rising patriotism of the era is indicated by the new prominence of Austrian artists. Gérard, Isabey, and Thomas Lawrence had been imported from France and England to document the events of the congress, but afterward local artists came into the fore. Fendi, Danhauser, Daffinger, Rudolf von Alt, and Ferdinand Waldmüller were commissioned for portraits; though these paintings are generally small, they share a highly finished painterly qual-

Wiener Moden.

*Wiener Moden.*

ity and regard for realism and detail. They reflect a time that was becoming conscious of its own merits and relishing its own achievements. Peter Krafft, though German born, was trained in both Vienna and Paris and became a true Austrian painter. In 1825 he received an important official commission for three monumental wall paintings illustrating the love of the Austrian people for their monarch. The programme for the paintings was determined by Empress Carolina Augusta herself; the subjects of the panels are events in the life of Franz I. Although Krafft's works depict events that occurred earlier in the century, between 1809 and 1814, he gives us a detailed account of life and fashions in the Vienna of the 1820s (Fig. 25). The streets are filled with officers in colorful uniforms and fantastic headgear, gentlemen in high-collared coats and long trousers waving their top hats in the air, and children in light dresses sashed at the waist with pantaloons peeping out from under the skirts.

The most interesting new development was in the style of the ladies' dresses. The silhouette had changed significantly since the beginning of the 1820s. The most noticeable change was the waistline, which had moved down to an almost natural position and was accented by a belt. The skirts, too, were cut much fuller and were still gathered at the back, but with a straight front. For streetwear in the 1820s darker colors, larger plaids, and stripes were preferred. The redingote changed, too; because of the fuller skirts, the *rotunde* —called a *Wickler* in Vienna—cut full and without a waist, enjoyed great popularity. The most popular outer garment, however, was the shawl. Beautiful cashmere shawls with paisley designs were first imported from India, but after 1812 they were also manufactured in Vienna. The Viennese manufacturer Arthaber began exporting shawls in 1825, and these fine woolen products remained one of Vienna's best luxury exports. Though they were called "Turkish shawls" in Vienna, to the rest of German-speaking Europe they were known as "Viennese shawls" (Fig. 24).

In their homes the ladies wore colorful little neckerchiefs with their light and low-cut negligées. The batiste example illustrated (Fig. 26) shows the Viennese

Fig. 28. Wilhelmine
Reichard, the first woman
to fly over Vienna in a
balloon. Lithograph, 1820.

predilection for beautiful embroidery and openwork on its long sleeves and on the flounces of its skirt. The elegant *Hausfrau* playing with her pet bird wears white gloves and a pretty lace bonnet in a room filled with flowers and light. The flower stand was an innovation of the Biedermeier furniture trade.

Viennese homelife impressed the visitors from abroad who were fortunate enough to be invited into the homes. Charles Sealsfield, an English traveler, reported from Vienna in 1823:

> A Viennese evening party in a small circle is undoubtedly the most charming way of passing the time. One comes together immediately after tea at six o'clock in the evening. Refreshments such as pineapple and grapes are handed around, and card games are organized. In the meantime a little orchestra plays pieces from operas by Mozart, Weber and Rossini, and if there are young girls in the house, a dance is quickly improvised.... These unpretentious, humble, really refined and simple people are much more inclined than others to enjoy the pleasures of life thoroughly....

Though Sealsfield described a soiree at the home of an aristocrat, the spirit of the evening was not unlike that of the famous "Schubertiaden." A circle of musicians, artists, literati, and amateurs whose central figure was the composer Franz Schubert gathered frequently at the homes of friends and patrons to read, play music, listen to Schubert's latest songs, and to dance (see Fig. 5). Moritz von Schwind, the renowned German romantic painter, spent much time in this circle and documented these gatherings for us; Schubert was inevitably at the piano, surrounded by a circle of pretty young ladies and aristocratic and "bohemian" young gentlemen listening attentively or dancing. Eduard Bauernfeld described such a gathering:

> Then there were the Schubert evenings, the so-called "Schubertiaden," where wine flowed in streams, the wonderful Vogl [a famous Viennese singer] performed all those magnificent songs, and poor Schubert! Franz had to accompany so much, that he could hardly control his short, fat fingers any longer. It was even worse for him at our own home ... where, however, there was no lack of charming ladies and girls. There our "Bertel," as we nicknamed him sometimes, had to play for us his latest waltzes and play and play until the long cotillion was over and the short, corpulent man, dripping with perspiration, could only recover during a simple supper.

Again and again contemporary documents confirm that life was simple in Vienna, but that seems never to have stopped anyone from having a good time. Although the ladies were dressed simply at the "Schubertiaden," they were resplendent in lovely evening gowns at the grand balls of *Fasching*, the carnival season that lasts from New Year's Eve until Lent. During the 1820s a great predilection for floral ornaments developed. These appeared not only as decor on the dresses, but particularly in women's coiffures (Fig. 27). During the day, instead of bonnets women wore enormous hats with wide brims and huge bows of ribbon on the crowns. Such hats were trimmed with an abundance of artificial flowers; sometimes whole branches or tall grasses were used. For evening wear the complicated chignons were engulfed in flowers and trimmings of the most imaginative kind. The most fashionable coiffeur and milliner in Vienna was Johann Langer. Almost all the coiffures and hats in the *Wiener Modenzeitung* are after his creations. For the most part, however, the milliners were women. These so-called *Modistinnen* sold ribbons and trims and could freshen up an old hat in the most fantastic manner. Tailoring, on the other hand, was strictly a man's profession, and it was not until 1844 that a woman, Maria Heinrich, was granted permission to run her own shop and to apprentice and train girls in cutting and sewing.

A charming lithograph made in 1820 (Fig. 28) honors Wilhelmine Reichard, the first woman to fly in a balloon over Vienna. The event put Vienna in league with London and Paris, the leading European centers of technological innovation. Another rather amusing example of "keeping abreast" is a dress designed by the Viennese couturier Beer, made up in an allover print of giraffes. The fabric design was created in honor of the first giraffes brought to Europe: one to Paris in 1826, and one to Vienna in 1827 as a gift from the pasha of Egypt to the emperor.

In the 1820s ladies started to wear jewelry again: small hanging earrings and delicate necklaces were popular, as were bracelets worn over short gloves. Prosperity had returned to Austria. A contemporary description of the state of the working class reads:

> To see torn or even damaged or dirty clothing is an absolute rarity. There is hardly a woman of the lower classes who doesn't have at least one article of clothing made of silk, be it a skirt, a corset or an apron; the majority even wear rich gold hats. The men are equally well dressed.

The gold hats—actually bonnets of linen and straw embroidered with gold sequins and metallic thread and trimmed with gold lace—were of Austrian and south German origin and were part of the peasant costume of these regions. The bonnets made in Linz were particularly splendid; because of their beauty they were taken over not only by rich peasant women, but also by the *Bürgermädchen*—the girls of the middle class in the cities—and enjoyed particular favor in Vienna. Like the Indian cashmere shawls and the passementerie taken from the hussar uniforms, the gold hats were another example of the clever Viennese adapting a foreign style to their own good use. Another case is that of Turkish slippers. As far back as the eighteenth century the embroidered slippers had been worn by men in the Balkan countries; in Vienna and to the west they were worn by ladies with their negligées.

The spirit in Austria after the congress was one of reconstruction and conservation. On the whole the emperor's subjects were loyal to him, although rivalries between the many different nationalities that made up the Austrian Empire were inevitable. It was not the emperor, but his chancellor, Metternich, who ordered strict surveillance and suppression of any democratic (revolutionary) activities. Censorship was extended not only to all written material, but even to beards in portraits, which could be considered revolutionary material! However, the revolution that brought down the French government in 1830 had only weak and belated repercussions in Austria. It was perhaps the unpreten-

tiousness of the Hapsburg rulers—the emperor's own thriftiness and simple humanity—that made for the good relations between the monarch and his people. Meanwhile, Louis-Philippe became known as the "bourgeois king," who carried an umbrella instead of the traditionally aristocratic sword. Contemporary portraits of the Hapsburg family (see Fig. 74) demonstrate how very bourgeois the imperial family wished themselves portrayed. A world of difference lies between these charming, intimate family scenes and the formal, utterly aristocratic portraits of Empress Maria Theresa and her family painted by Füger or Meytens (see Fig. 61).

At court there was a strict dress code in effect. It dictated the proper dress for grand galas, little galas, coronations, and periods of mourning. Some of the most beautiful creations of the Viennese couturiers are the "Hungarian" gala dresses. The silhouette of these changed with the development of fashion over the decades, but the essential elements remained the same: the laced bodice, the apron of embroidered gauze, the long, trained skirt (court etiquette in the nineteenth century always required a train, though the length might vary), and a veil held by a diadem. The Hungarian gala dresses were always richly embroidered in gold and silver tinsel and sequins and were among the most lavish and glorious dresses ever designed.

As far as fashion was concerned, however, the court—the empress—did not set the trend in Austria. The true creators of fashion in the 1830s were the queens of the stage in Vienna as well as in London and Paris. In fact during the thirties Viennese couturiers again became dependent on French fashions. The *Wiener Theater Zeitung*, first published in 1832, reported and illustrated the latest trends in Paris in an effort to rival the very successful *Wiener Modenzeitung*, which itself included reports from Paris after 1834. The illustrations in the *Wiener Modenzeitung* were drawn after original designs by the Viennese couturiers Beer, Petko, and Joseph Gunkel, but the style of the drawings is French.

The basic change in ladies' fashion in the first half of

THE IMPERIAL STYLE

Fig. 29. *Portrait of Dr.
Josef August Eltz with his
wife, Caroline, and his
eight children at Ischl.
Oil on canvas, 1835, by
Ferdinand Georg Waldmül-
ler. Österreichische
Galerie, Vienna.*

the 1830s was the increased volume of forms: the sleeves as well as the skirts became fuller and fuller, while the size of the playful ornaments was much reduced. Skirts were left completely unadorned, and all the attention was focused on the bodice and the sleeves. The long, puffed sleeves soon grew into "leg-of-mutton" sleeves, and were even further inflated into what the Viennese called "elephant sleeves." These were set in very low at the shoulder and supported by little down-filled pillows or fishbone cages tied to the upper arms. The waist—tightly corseted—seemed diminutive compared to the broad expanse of sleeve and décolleté and the full skirt. The fabrics preferred in the 1830s were darker and heavier than those seen in the early years of the Biedermeier. The headgear also changed: the enormous hats of the 1820s were replaced by bonnets, most of them made of fine Florentine straw. The brim no longer hid the face, but surrounded it. The ribbons were allowed to float freely instead of being tied anxiously under the chin as they had been earlier. The fashion plates of these years show the popularity of ribbons, which were used in all shades and colors to decorate the bonnets, to wear as belts, and to trim every part of a costume. The extreme proportions of the sleeves made new outer garments necessary. The waisted coat came into fashion. Another outer garment, the collarlike mantelet, enjoyed great popularity, too, holding a place next to the never-discarded shawl. Outerwear became increasingly important as Austrians discovered the outdoor life. It became the custom to leave the hot and dusty city during the summer months and move to the country. Ferdinand Waldmüller's portrait of the Eltz family at Ischl (Fig. 29) conveys a sense of the high value the Biedermeier placed on family life. The painting is also a realistic document of the fashion of the mid-1830s. Waldmüller, by all accounts a dandy himself, can always be trusted to be absolutely correct in the way he treated fashion in his portraits. Hardly a painter has ever striven for naturalism as much as he; even if the poses of the sitters seem theatrical and contrived, the details are undoubtedly as he saw them. He even painted the creases left in the silk dresses from the way they were folded in the closets!

THE IMPERIAL STYLE

The year 1835 represented a turning point in politics as well as in fashion in Austria. Emperor Franz I died, and his son Ferdinand I was made his successor even though he was incompetent to rule. The government actually slipped more than ever into the hands of Chancellor Metternich, who was nicknamed "Fürst von Mitternacht" ("the Duke of Midnight") because of his widespread network of secret police who monitored radical movements. In the arts as well as in fashion the year brought significant changes. In the decorative arts (furniture, glassware, porcelain) the straight and simple lines of the early Biedermeier were abandoned for a more playful and curvilinear style that became known as "second Rococo." The same trend occurred in fashion. The gargantuan sleeves could not grow any larger—no more material could possibly be supported by the fishbone constructions—and were therefore suddenly abandoned. One of the first examples of the new type of sleeve, called *à la jardinière*, was seen in a fashion plate in the *Wiener Modenzeitung* titled "Gaze Elssler." It is a dress of yellow silk, with short, tight sleeves ruched just below the shoulder, a broad décolleté that leaves the shoulders bare, and a tight bodice ending in a pointed waist that lies over the full skirt very gracefully. At the décolleté and at the hem are bouquets of purple velvet buttercups. This very charming creation was named after Vienna's brightest star of the stage, the internationally acclaimed dancer Fanny Elssler. She represents all the grace and charm of her age. Like her colleagues in Paris and London, she became one of the trend setters of European fashion. Her "Cachucha," a dance of Spanish flavor, became the sensation of Paris and Vienna and even America. Fanny's success can be gathered from a contemporary description of a performance:

> In eight performances Fanny danced the Cachucha twenty-two times, yet who can boast that he knows this dance completely or can say that the twenty-second performance was not just as interesting as the first.... I have been present at many a stormy evening in the theater, but I have never witnessed such general and unrestrained excitement as at [her] last appearance....

The "Cachucha" costume, a dress of pink satin trimmed with black lace on the bodice and skirt (Fig. 31) was designed by the Viennese couturier Beer and was soon adapted for the wardrobes of the Viennese ladies. It was only natural that the darling of Vienna was a dancer. Never had dance mania been as pronounced anywhere as it was in Vienna during the Biedermeier. Dances at home or in dance halls like the renowned Apollo Saal had been popular in Vienna even before the congress. Here ländler, *Galops*, and *Langaus*, were danced with much abandon. The *Langaus* was finally prohibited by law because so many young couples contracted pneumonia due to overexertion.

It was, however, the Viennese waltz, the most graceful and romantic of all ballroom dances, that was the ultimate product of the Biedermeier era. Although Mozart and Schubert had written waltzes, the composers who really perfected this dance form were Johann Strauss the Elder, Josef Lanner, and, finally the greatest of them all Johann Strauss the Younger. Lanner and the elder Strauss had been composing and performing throughout the 1820s, and when Chopin visited Vienna in 1830 he remarked in a letter: "Lanner and Strauss and their waltz dominate everything." The popularity of this revolutionary dance—the first socially acceptable contact dance—can be gathered from the following figures: during the carnival season of 1832, 277 balls were attended by 200,000 persons, roughly half the population of Vienna! Strauss senior was the first real producer of huge public parties in dance halls or out of doors. His evenings at "Sperl's" or in the Prater, Vienna's largest park, had such romantic themes as "A Night in Venice," "Flower Carnival," and "Banquet in Paradise." No expense was spared on the lavish decor of flowers, lanterns, and even artificial canals. The evenings, featuring the highly trained Strauss orchestra, became renowned as the most romantic and exciting entertainments in all of Europe. Strauss's compositions document the events of his day: the "Eisenbahn Lust" honors the opening of the first railroad in Austria in 1837; the "Cachucha Galop" is a tribute to Fanny Elssler. But more often than not, Strauss's inspiration was a beautiful Viennese lady. How striking these ladies must have been is well documented in the pages of the *Wiener Modenzeitung*, which are filled with the most bewitching and romantic creations. Light in color and spirit, the pretty dresses are enhanced by radiant faces framed by the most fanciful arrangements of flowers in the coiffures.

Besides being zealous dancers, the Viennese were also avid theater goers. It is not surprising that the most typically Viennese plays, written by Raimund, Nestroy, and Grillparzer, were produced during the 1830s. Social criticism, particularly criticism of the government and the Church, was strictly forbidden and censored, but through double entendres and subtlety, the playwrights conveyed their meaning amusingly. Theater began to exert a tremendous influence on fashion during the thirties. The popular plays of the day, such as Adolph Bäuerle's *Rococo*, expressed a great nostalgia for the vanished glamour of the courts of Europe in the eighteenth century and for the playfulness of the Rococo period. Often it was the sets and costumes, designed by Viennese artists and couturiers, that excited the fancy of the audience—not the play itself.

Neo-Rococo forms were enthusiastically taken up in fashion (Fig. 30). Skirts, which had become floor length and full all around during the first half of the 1830s, became so full that in 1838 Beer followed his Parisian colleagues' lead and cut his first crinoline. The wide skirts were open in front over a petticoat in imitation of the eighteenth-century styles. The bodices of the dresses remained close-fitting, the *corsage à la vierge* or "bertha" being the most popular form of décolleté. The waist was cut in a point, again in imitation of a Rococo form, which made a flattering transition to the full skirt. The sleeves took several shapes: short and puffed or sometimes gathered up to reveal imitation *engageants* (white lace ruffles, imitations of the trimmings on Rococo dresses). The preferred materials were also reminiscent of those worn in the eighteenth century: silks, brocades, and velvets in white or pastels, embellished with delicate embroidery or woven floral patterns. Everything was light and charming. Accessories like fans, purses, and folding umbrellas were diminutive and expressed pure coquetry, just as they had done

in the eighteenth century. The coiffures changed again, too. The hair was still parted in the center, but the complicated chignons of the earlier Biedermeier gave way to three or four ringlets falling from the temples, a style that remained popular for many years to come and to us is the very essence of Biedermeier coiffure.

The nostalgia for the Rococo expressed the popular wish to escape the dire realities of the day. By 1840 industrialization had left its mark on Vienna as it had on the other European capitals. The population had doubled within thirty years, growing from 224,548 in 1810 to 431,147 by 1840; the increased ranks of the proletariat had brought to Vienna the same problems that were rampant in Paris and London. Though Vienna lagged behind these cities in new industries, it had a very productive furniture industry, and its piano makers, such as the houses of Streicher and Bösendorfer, were world renowned. Wool and raw silk products, however, were still the major export articles of the Biedermeier era. Yet the financial state of the monarchy remained critical. In 1840 the financial power was in the hands of the great bankers like the Rothschilds, while seventy percent of the population still depended on an agricultural economy. The decline of the welfare of the working classes is amply documented by series of graphic illustrations, the *Kaufrufe* (street cries), made by different artists between the last quarter of the eighteenth century and 1848 (Fig. 32). Here the "common" people—street vendors, washerwomen, tobacconists, and the other tradespeople—are portrayed. Their appearance declined noticeably during the 1830s and 40s. Growing public dissatisfaction and the struggle for rights and recognition by the various ethnic groups that constituted the Austrian state hung like a threatening cloud over the empire.

The fashion plates in the *Wiener Modenzeitung* show a loss of confidence in the distinctive Viennese style during the 1830s and 40s. The Viennese couturiers Bohlinger, Beer, Brünner, and others now made annual trips to Paris to faithfully copy the Parisian originals in order to guarantee the Viennese clientele that they were truly au courant. Even the format of the fashion plates and their design conformed to that of the French

publications; the ladies were shown in sketchy interiors or hastily drawn landscapes with much more emphasis given to the mise-en-scène than to the details of the clothes. The day dresses shown were of less expensive materials, such as mixtures of silks and cotton, organdies, and chiffons; large plaids, and colorful striped materials replaced delicate floral designs. For evening wear the dresses were of more sumptuous materials than ever: velvets, moirés, silks, brocades, and tulles. The cut had not changed markedly since the late thirties, though the trimmings constantly varied. The bodice remained tight, and the pointed waist also continued to be popular. The Neo-Rococo skirts with open fronts were discarded in favor of skirts decorated with flounces. The dresses and evening coats worn to the theater were often made of such materials as *changeant* silks, which reflected the newly installed gaslights; it was a typical example of fashion adapting to the innovations of the time. Ferdinand Waldmüller, in his portrait of a young lady at her dressing table (Fig. 33), also knew how to capture the play of light over the deep folds of a beautiful cream silk dress and to enhance its sensuous quality, set off by the red cashmere shawl the young lady is about to drape around herself. The young woman portrayed is a typical Viennese *süsses Mädel*—a girl full of warmth, charm, and unaffected sweetness. If one compares this portrait to that of the Comtesse d'Haussonville painted by the brilliant French artist Ingres a few years later (Fig. 34), the difference between the French and Austrian ideal becomes obvious. The French lady is pensive, aloof, thoroughly urbane, and a little cold. The Austrian girl seems naive, spontaneous, and simple. This is not to say that Vienna or the Viennese were any less cultivated than Paris or the Parisians. As a matter of fact, an event that occurred in 1844 secured Vienna's position as one of the most attractive cities in Europe. The debut of Johann Strauss the Younger, Europe's "waltz king," was attended by the cream of Viennese society and was the social sensation of the year. From then on, Vienna had two Strausses, and the competition between father and son divided the city. The public, of course, gained from the rivalry. The younger Strauss was soon the idol of the

Fig. 35. An emancipated
Viennese woman in her
boudoir. Detail of a crayon
lithograph, about 1855, by
F. Leybold. Museen der
Stadt Wien.

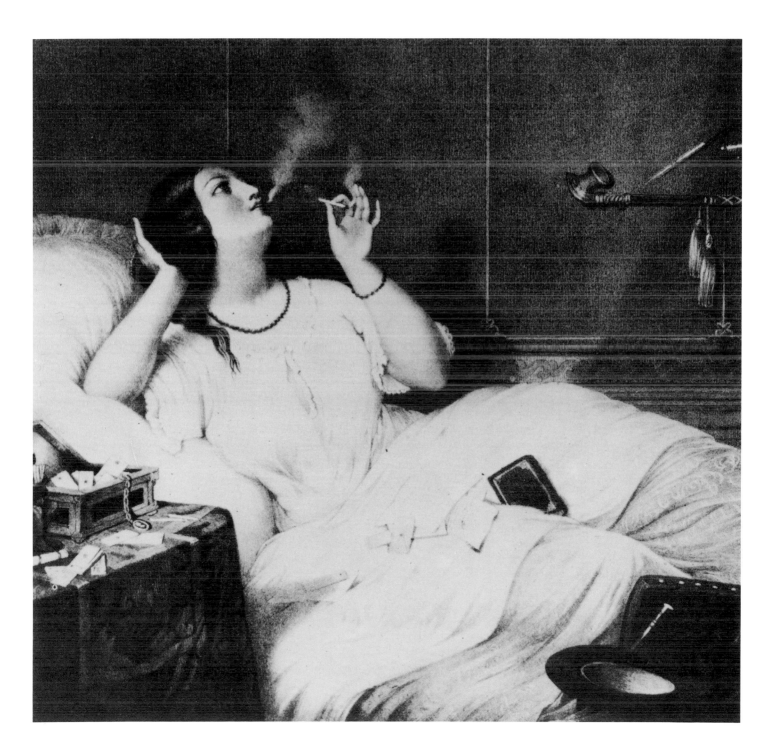

ladies of Vienna; his gypsy-like good looks, his fiery temperament, and his virtuosity made him the darling of the city. It was above all the *jeunesse dorée*, the beautiful young people, who made up his followers. Wilhelm von Kaulbach wrote of Strauss's importance in Vienna, "... Vienna is a city of sensuous pleasure, and Strauss is the sun around which everything revolves."

Fever-pitch entertainments and new sensations like the performances of the "Swedish Nightingale," Jenny Lind, appealed to the by now very refined Viennese audiences. Jenny's success was attributed equally to her voice and her elaborate costumes, which, like Fanny Elssler's, inspired the fashions of the day. Costumes from Jenny's actual theatrical wardrobe can be found among the fashion plates of the *Wiener Modenzeitung*. Yet the general air of depression made itself felt even in the gaiety of the balls. According to a contemporary description, the carnival season of 1847 was clouded over by a tired, listless mood. The first rumblings of the revolution of 1848 could be heard on all sides. The revolution, a bloody uprising of the proletariat, supported by liberal students, was not as violent in Vienna as it was in France, but the situation, exacerbated by ethnic uprisings in other parts of the empire, was critical enough to cause the emperor to temporarily abandon Vienna and the Hofburg.

The upheaval, though not strong enough to overthrow the government, had a significant influence on society and fashion. The changes it brought were by no means as radical as those the French Revolution had initiated half a century earlier. During the days of riots the Viennese women who sympathized with the cause took to the streets and barricades in "Kalabreser" hats—men's soft, wide-brimmed felt hats also worn by German and Italian revolutionaries—or in students' caps, also symbols of democratic convictions. They decorated themselves with military accouterments and—most shocking of all—smoked cigars (Fig. 35)! When the revolution had been subdued and law and order was once again established, there was a curious standstill in fashion. Simple, unobtrusive styles were preferred; the playful, aristocratic forms of the Rococo were given up altogether, and richly embroidered

materials were discarded in favor of more discreet decorations (Fig. 36). The palette—if one can speak of a palette in fashion—also became sober and muted. (It is interesting to note than from 1848 on, men wore coats and pants of the same material: the business suit was born.) The luxurious *Wiener Modenzeitung* did not survive the revolution. Its successor, the new fashion magazine *L'Iris*, published in Paris, began printing dress patterns. Now the woman of the working class could aspire to wear the same style clothes as a grand lady.

The Viennese Biedermeier era really came to an end with the revolution of 1848. The accession of eighteen-year-old Emperor Franz Joseph I initiated a new epoch in the history of the Austrian Empire. His long reign and forceful personality dominated the social and cultural life of the fading Hapsburg Empire until World War I. Although the spirit of conservatism continued to pervade Austrian politics and society, conditions were not the same as they had been before the revolution. The simplicity and quiet serenity of the Biedermeier was abruptly over.

Otto Wagner, the famous Viennese architect of the early twentieth century, wrote on the relationship of taste, fashion, and art and asserted that man's appearance—the shape, color, and decoration of his clothes—always corresponds exactly to the artistic spirit of his time. To hardly a moment in history could Wagner's thesis be better applied than to the Viennese Biedermeier. Artists like M. M. Daffinger worked as designers; couturiers worked for the theaters; influences were closely related and crossed frequently. The development of the Viennese Biedermeier fashion truly parallels the history and the stylistic development of contemporary art. After 1815 the great thrust had been toward independence, toward breaking away from foreign fashion dictatorship. The *Wiener Modenzeitung* had at first published only local creations, as if to echo the political slogan "Away from Paris," which was heard everywhere. Vienna had always been in the mainstream of European developments; its geographical position between East and West made it a natural juncture for the meeting of many different traditions and customs. At a time when Vienna's artists seemed to

express themselves best on a small scale (Schubert wrote hundreds of songs, yet left his symphonies unfinished; painters perfected the miniature portrait and delighted in small genre scenes), a parallel predilection for exquisite detail was the outstanding feature of Viennese fashion. The true climax of the Viennese Biedermeier, in art as well as in fashion, occurred during the 1820s. After that Vienna slowly ceased to lead in the development of fashion, yielding once again to Paris, whose dictatorship continued until the turn of the twentieth century. In about 1900 the artists of the Viennese Secession began a concerted effort to reestablish a distinctive Viennese style. The fashion as well as the art of the Wiener Werkstätte derived inspiration from the rich tradition of the glorious past. The Viennese Biedermeier fashions—their graceful designs, lovingly executed details, and fine workmanship—reflect a time in which life was simple and unhurried—an era that was totally civilized and, above all, secure.

THE IMPERIAL STYLE

Fig. 37. *The waltz à la mode. Waltzing in London. Lithograph, about 1850. Museen der Stadt Wien.*

# Waltz Interlude

By Ruth Katz, Professor of Musicology,
Hebrew University, Jerusalem

Dance, like other art forms, often reflects the values and social relations of its time and place. The rural American square dance, with couples of all ages do-si-doing their partners and bowing to their corners, expressed in choreography a society in which each household needed a hard-working man and woman, and the help of neighbors, to survive. When ceremonies include hundreds of people dancing together, as they do in many parts of New Guinea, the community is usually valued above the individual.

Dance also reflects historical change. The upheavals of late eighteenth-century Europe, when industrialization and the French Revolution thrust the West into the modern era, are clearly recorded in the dances of the time. A comparison of the courtly minuet, which preceded the French Revolution, and the waltz of the 1800s is almost like a sociological analysis of the two contrasting societies in which these dances prevailed.

The minuet, danced only by the nobility, was a restrained expression of the classical values of clarity, balance, and regularity. Although it appeared simple, its intricate steps had to be studied before it could be executed in public, and there existed a number of manuals to explain its rules. Dancing masters from England to Italy spent hours with aristocratic students instructing them in the fine distinctions between the spread, the leg cross, and the final.

But the minuet was also a performance. As Goethe said, "Nobody ventures unconcernedly to dance unless he has been taught the art; the minuet, in particular, is regarded as a work of art and is performed, indeed, only by a few couples. The couples are surrounded by the rest of the company, admired and applauded at the end." The admiring onlookers, who represented the community of European nobility, were also a part of the minuet.

The protocol of the minuet reflected the social rank of the dancers. Hosts carefully researched the background of each guest to determine who would open the ball and in what order each guest would step out onto the floor. The dance was a ritualized reenactment of the world; and its formality and uniformity made it possible to vividly represent subtle distinctions of rank.

The waltz, in contrast, was a dance of the people, by the people, and for the people. Everyone danced the waltz. In 1814 the Congress of Vienna met to reestablish political order in Europe after Napoleon's disastrous attempt to destroy the royal houses of the western hemisphere and to establish his own imperial domain. The congress brought together not only the diplomats and delegates of different nationalities but also representatives of different social classes. There were aristocrats of the old regime as well as merchants, artisans, and industrialists who were imbued with post-Revolutionary political and social ideas. The passion for waltzing knew neither political nor social boundaries.

The rage for the waltz so swept the Vienna Congress onto its feet that it was said in Europe, "The Congress doesn't talk, it dances." Enthusiasm for the waltz was shared by kings and commoners. The monarchs of France, Prussia, and Russia invited Johann Strauss, Sr., to introduce his music to their courts, and as many as six thousand people waltzed nightly at the Apollo Palace in Vienna. The building contained five large dancing rooms and thirty-one smaller rooms, including a hall for pregnant women, who, while segregating themselves with modesty, did not want to lose a moment of dancing.

The success of the waltz as a dance form was matched by its success as a purely musical form. Concert performances of waltz music attracted large audiences not only to the ballrooms and to "pop" concerts but to the very halls in which Beethoven's music had been performed the night before.

About the middle of the eighteenth century a new nationalism was evolving. The middle classes began to define themselves as active participants in a political, economic, and cultural unit—the nation—and not simply as subjects of the king.

In the quest for their national origins, people looked to the folk dance. The whirling dances were rediscovered and became fashionable in middle- and upper-class society. Paul Nettl tells about the triumph of the age-old German folk dance, the Dreher, which quickly moved onto the dance floor and even into musical compositions. The ländler had a similar success.

Fig. 38. The grand galop danced to the music of Johann Strauss the Elder. The Galop *was thought to have originated in Hungary and reached the height of its popularity in western Europe in the 1830s. It was a rapid form of the polka, danced in 2/4 time. Often it was used to conclude other formal dances.*

Colored engraving, by A. Geiger, published in the Wiener Theater Zeitung *of June 26, 1839. Museen der Stadt Wien.*

THE IMPERIAL STYLE

Fig. 39. *The modern galop, or "dancing into eternity." Detail of a colored etching, published in 1838 in the magazine* Hans Jörgl. *Museen der Stadt Wien. Inv. no. 97.116/21.*

Fig. 40. *Detail of a nineteenth-century cartoon by W. Grogler titled "Viennese waltzes." Museen der Stadt Wien.*

*Fig. 42. The ballroom in
the old Elysium dance hall.
Detail of a lithograph, by
Franz Wolf. Museen der
Stadt Wien.*

THE IMPERIAL STYLE

Of the many whirling dances it was the ländler, combined with some elements of the Schleifer, that defined the waltz. In the ländler the couples followed a circular course while turning, in close embrace, to each two measures of music. Most ländlers were in three-four rhythm with a strongly accentuated first beat, just as the waltz was to be. But the ländler had skips and turnings-under-the-arm that were abandoned in the waltz in favor of gliding the feet along the floor in the style of the Schleifer. This glide, in place of the freer but less sensuous skip, makes for the smooth turning and "letting go" for which the waltz is famous. The German word *Walzen*, apparently derived from the Latin *volvere*, to turn around, was introduced in the mid-1700s.

The waltz is best characterized by individual expression. There were no rules to memorize, only a few basic steps to learn, and individuals were encouraged to develop their own variations. The dancers surrendered their worldly identities upon entering the society of the dance, a society that was altogether different from the world outside the ballroom. Recognition in the dance was not a reiteration of the dancer's status in the world, but a reward for excellent performance in the make-believe society of the ballroom. Although there were no onlookers, on occasion the best couples brought the evening to a close while the other dancers encircled them to confer recognition. The emphasis was on the participation of all, the equality of all, and the liberty of all.

The beautiful commoner, if she waltzed very well, might be invited to dance with the prince. This aspect of the waltz mirrored the rewards offered by the new society for achievement instead of birthright.

General public support of art soon took the place of aristocratic patronage, and with this change, music moved out of the courts and drawing rooms and into concert halls. These were the settings for the performance of emotional, sentimental, and individualistic nineteenth-century music that represents the predominance of middle-class values. The waltz was part of this movement. Ultimately the cult of sensibility ensnared the aristocracy itself: middle-class romanticism reached

Fig. 43. Ball at court.
Gouache on paper, 1900,
by Wilhelm Gause. Museen
der Stadt Wien. Photo:
Lynton Gardiner, Photo-
graph Studio, The Metro-
politan Museum of Art,
New York.

THE IMPERIAL STYLE

upward to the waning aristocracy and downward to the industrial social classes. By the middle of the nineteenth century the reinstated royal family of France had become a portrait of this changed world view. Louis-Philippe, who became king in 1830, was known for his bourgeois clothes and manner and his dedication to the waltz.

But the transition from the aristocratic monarchy of Louis XVI to the bourgeois state of Louis-Philippe was by no means easy. The waltz became popular at a time when the old social order was crumbling. From 1792 to 1814, Austria was at war no less than five times. Large armies moved back and forth across Europe. Napoleon invaded Russia in 1812 with an army of six hundred thousand men, of whom only a fraction returned. People fled their homes in order to avoid battle zones. Peasants left the countryside for the cities and the New World, and many died from the new diseases of the expanding industrial society. In all, a sense of displacement prevailed as the security of having a fixed and proper place in a structured society gave way.

*Gemütlichkeit* was one response to this situation. Individuals sought good cheer and camaraderie and allowed themselves the luxury of self-indulgence and

Fig. 45. *Johann Strauss being crowned waltz king of the world and observed by an august assembly of fellow composers. Drawing, 1899, by Theo Zasche. Austrian National Library, Vienna*

JOHANN STRAUSS, DER WALZERKÖNIG.

the taste of new experience. They sought to cope with uncertainty not so much by forging a new reality as by slipping off into a dream. Losing oneself in the waltz was one of the most exquisite expressions of this process of escape.

The suspension of time and the giddy experience were essential elements of the waltz craze of the nineteenth century. The thrilling whirl into a private world of sensuality was appropriate to the harsh reality of a troubled world without standards, a world in which the individual had to find his way. In *The Sorrows of Young Werther*, Goethe's romantic hero confesses to Wilhelm that while waltzing with Lotte everything around him seemed to disappear. "I was no longer human," he says, "with that lovely creature in my arms, flying with her like the wind so that everything around disappeared."

Yet there was also a centripetal force at work. While the waltz threatened to hurl the dancers into space, the support of one's partner provided tangible assurance. In the security of one's partner's arms still another kind of liberty could be taken, the kind against which the clergymen had warned.

Sensuality and heretofore unknown erotic license pervaded the world of the waltz. Reality was suspended for a moment, and responsibility was discarded. Objectivity, formality, detachment, and deference, all so characteristic of the demanding minuet, were put aside; the experience of self and self-involvement in an equal and fraternal world—at once secure and thrilling—animated the dancers and reflected the frustrated aspirations of the times.

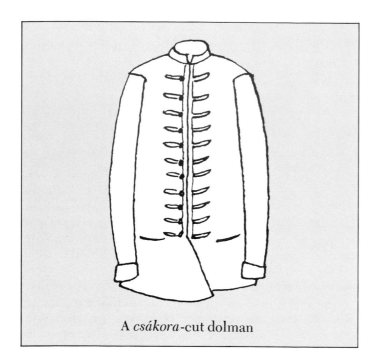

A *csákora*-cut dolman

## GLOSSARY

### CSÁKORA CUT
A style of tailoring the flared area below the waist of a dolman. A diagonally cut piece of fabric overlaps the front of the garment.

### DOLMAN
A coat or jacket worn under a *mente*. It is cut straight from the shoulder seams or fitted to the waist, from which it flares out. Fastened with loops and buttons.

### MENTE
An outercoat, often trimmed with fur, cut straight from the shoulder seams to the waist, then flaring out to end at the knees or calves.

### PÁRTA
A woman's cap made of tinsel.

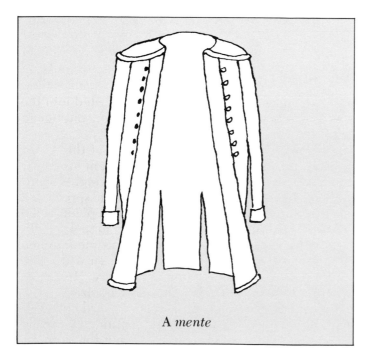

A *mente*

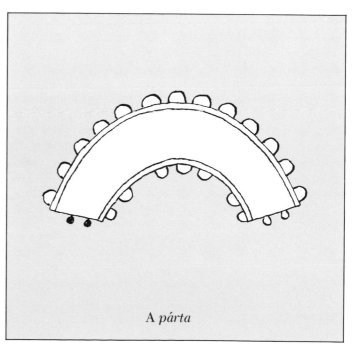

A *párta*

# How the Hungarian National Costume Evolved

By Katalin Földi-Dózsa, Curator of Textiles,
The Hungarian National Museum, Budapest

*"The Magyars are a very appealing and beautiful people. . . . Their clothes are made of brocade."*
— Abdul Gardīzī,
an eleventh-century Persian historian

Under the leadership of Árpád, the Magyars entered the Carpathian basin in A.D. 896 and wandered into Hungary through what are now the southern steppes of Russia. There are no images of these ancient people; only through asides in the histories of other ancient tribes and through the remains in their graves do we have any conception of the way they lived. They apparently dressed like eastern horsemen — much the way modern nomads in the Middle and Far East still do. The most important item of their clothing was a knee-length caftan with a stand-up collar and a slit opening in the front that was either laced closed or fastened with buttons.

Fur trapping and leather tanning were highly developed industries among the Magyars. They wore leather hats and protected their feet by lashing a strip of leather to them with leather thongs. The most affluent horsemen wore silks and gold-patterned brocades; their humbler countrymen wore homemade hemp cloth or, in the winter, heavy felt. Magyar battle gear was light, sewn leather. Their pointed leather hats and winter outercoats were trimmed with fur.

The most impressive item in the Magyar costume was an elaborate leather belt laden with gold and stamped silver. It not only held together their loose garments but was also a place to carry valuables: eastern-style bent blades, gold-encrusted cartridge cases, bow cases, and fire irons were all hung from the belt. The belt itself was lavishly decorated with metal plates suspended from leather straps. When a man walked, these ornaments — and his assorted possessions — clanged together. To further enhance their dazzling appearance, the ancient Magyars wore opulent rings and earrings; brooches and buttons were finely made by their nomadic goldsmiths.

The Magyars shaved their heads, except for three long "ponytails," one at the crown of the head and one at either temple. These were braided and held together with a metal hoop. The hairstyle naturally evoked much comment in Europe, where it was considered paganistic. However, in spite of religious reservations, the style soon spread, and by the twelfth and thirteenth centuries it was in use as far away as the German border. As late as the nineteenth century men in remote villages — especially shepherds — wore this unique coiffure

The women wore a *párta*, or headdress, adorned with metal plates, and metal disks hung from it by ribbons or leather strips. The hems of their knee-length skirts were similarly decorated. Over her skirt a woman wore a cape that closed in the front or at the sides and pants and soft leather boots. Except for her *párta*, she dressed very much like a man, even wearing the same elaborately crafted jewelry.

The lightly clad Magyar horsemen successfully looted and terrorized neighboring settlements at the turn of the tenth century. "Lord, save us from the arrows of the Magyars," was the alarmed expression heard in the villages of the Danube basin. During this period the Magyar warriors ranged as far as the northern borders of Germany, returning with sacks of booty. In time, however, the Germans used the interlopers' own tactics against them and defeated them at Augsburg in 955. The broken people were then faced with a dilemma: stop their wandering and wait for their religious and social customs to be assimilated into the feudal Christian culture around them — or continue to loot.

Géza (ruled 970–997), a descendant of the Árpád dynasty, put an end to the raids. To augment his power he surrounded himself with German knights, converted to Christianity, and invited priests to spread that religion throughout his land. His son Stephen (ruled 997–1038) continued his father's efforts to seek an alliance with the Germans and bring his people into line with the culture of western Europe. In A.D. 1000 Stephen became the first king of Hungary. His crown was a gift from the pope; later he was canonized.

The shift to a new nonsecular life-style did not occur smoothly, and looting and fighting continued for many years. The new order also brought about the suppres-

THE IMPERIAL STYLE

Fig. 46. *Embroidered roundel portraying King Stephen I of Hungary. Detail of Stephen's canonization cope made in 1031, thirty years after he took the throne. Hungarian National Museum, Budapest.*

Fig. 47. *Detail from the title page of a picture chronicle made during the reign of King Louis Nagy (1342–82). The mix of eastern- and western-style clothes worn by the men at left and right shows that styles from the East as well as from Europe were fashionable at the Hungarian court. Hungarian National Museum, Budapest.*

Fig. 48. *Portrait of King Matthias Corvinus (reigned 1458–90). By Mantegna(?). The king is shown wearing the fur-trimmed overcoat that was the forerunner of the Hungarian mente. Hungarian National Museum, Budapest.*

sion of the old styles of dress and the active promotion of western fashions. The king and his court naturally set the standard. Wide shirts and western armor soon replaced the caftan. Most people emulated the king's taste, although the occasional Byzantine costume was also seen.

According to old records, the Hungarian king's canonization cope was sewn by the nuns of Vesprem County in the year 1031 under the supervision of Stephen's wife, Gisela. The cope was originally meant to be a priest's robe. In an embroidered roundel on the garment itself Stephen is shown dressed in a wide, tunic-type dress and decorative, round-collared cope (Fig. 46). This costume typifies the Byzantine influence on eastern European styles.

After Stephen's death the Byzantine influence grew stronger, since later rulers began to trade with the eastern empire for silk and other precious commodities. By the mid-eleventh century everyone in the upper classes wore a variation of the same costume, a long-sleeved shirtlike garment worn with a buckled cape, although the peasants and lesser nobility were slow to change from their caftans and pointed fur hats. The richness of decorative details varied according to the wearer's affluence. Flax and hemp cloth were made locally, but broadcloth was imported from Ghent and Ypres. Scarlet cloth was brought in from Byzantium, and silks and damasks came from Lucca, Milan, and Florence or from the East.

In 1241 a new tribe from the East, the Tartars, swept into Hungary. They wore no armor and defeated the heavily clad Magyars by outmaneuvering them, just as the Magyars themselves had defeated the western tribes three centuries earlier. The Tartars pillaged Hungary in 1242 and headed home. Another eastern tribe, the Kuns, who had been fleeing the Tartars, found themselves stranded among the Magyars in the Danube-Tisza valley. The Kuns were good fighters and offered to help Béla, then king of Hungary, with the reconstruction of his ravaged land. The Kuns' dress was similar to that of the ancient Magyars, and their appearance after the Tartar invasion sparked a revival of the old styles. Once again one saw pointed caps and caftans

at court, despite the outrage such apparel caused the Christians. The king was in favor of Kun dress, which naturally became firmly entrenched. The most notable contribution of the Kuns was a new style of headdress with horns protruding from either side.

An illustrated chronicle prepared during the reign of King Louis Nagy (1342–82) documents the harmony in which eastern and western styles coexisted in Hungary. The king is shown on the title page of the chronicle wearing the most fashionable European style of his era and flanked by noblemen in western armor and others wearing form-fitting caftans (Fig. 47). One caftan style involved folding the front over to one side in a double-breasted effect that perfectly demonstrated the marriage of eastern and European influences in Hungarian dress.

In 1974 archaeologists discovered a cache of statues buried in the courtyard of Buda Castle. Many of the figures, made between 1370 and 1382, represent horsemen wearing western-style clothing. The discovery adds strength to the theory that the Hungarian nobility of the fourteenth and fifteenth centuries dressed very much like their counterparts in France, Germany, Poland, and Czechoslovakia.

The golden age of Hungarian history coincided with the reign of King Matthias Cornivus (1458–90). Matthias was a famous Turk-fighter and wealthy landowner who bound his country closer to Italy by marrying Beatrix, the daughter of the king of Naples. Soon cultural and economic ties developed between Hungary and Italy, whose Renaissance tastes were the most progressive in Europe.

Detailed accounts survive of the lavish festivities staged at Matthias's court. When the king went to meet his bride his entourage "glittered with gold, silver, and precious stones. Ten huge steeds ridden by pages wearing yellow, gray, green, and brown velvet preceded the king." During the wedding ceremony Matthias wore his crown and a cape embroidered with precious stones and pearls and awed everyone in attendance with his splendor. The nobility eagerly imitated their leader and ordered silks and velvets from Florence, Ferrara, and Milan. Miklós Ujlaki appeared

Fig. 49. *Portrait of a Hungarian nobleman wearing a short-sleeved dolman over an embroidered shirt. Hungarian National Museum, Budapest.*

at court in an outfit adorned with no fewer than five hundred jewels.

The Hungarians eagerly adopted the new Italian styles, especially the shirt. This was usually made of fine white linen with decorative embroidery on the wide sleeves and high collar. Young men wore a form-fitting waistcoat over the shirt, with sleeves slashed to the elbow to reveal the embroidery on their shirt sleeves. Older men who lacked the physique to sport such a revealing garment usually wore conservative knee-length greatcoats open in the front. Out of respect for his bride, however, Matthias had worn the Italian-ate waistcoat at his wedding, although it was covered by his royal robes. Most men wore a robelike coat with a fur-trimmed collar over the greatcoat. Matthias must have favored this style, as all surviving portraits show him wearing it (Fig. 48).

Beatrix and her ladies-in-waiting clung to the styles from their native Italy. Their damask or brocade skirts were sewn to high bodices, and the sleeves were slit to allow free movement of the arms. A woman of the court wore a wide cape and one of several different head-dresses: a fillet, a hairnet, a *párta*, or perhaps simply jewelry. Magyar-style clothing had already begun to be reserved for holidays or special occasions: Matthias sent his son's Italian fiancée, Bianca Maria Sforza, Magyar dresses and jewelry as engagement presents.

The golden age was short-lived. After the fifteenth century, especially after the death of Matthias, the Hungarian borders were constantly threatened by the Turks. The Magyars, in heavy western-style armor, were no match for the lightly clad Turks. The most important Hungarian victories were the ones fought by the deft hussars, a light cavalry unit that had never before been considered first-rank fighters. *Huszár* is a Balkan word that filtered into Hungarian through the Slavic languages. The nomadic hussars were widely thought to be wandering vandals, but in 1481 Matthias designated them the third branch of his fighting force, ranking just below his infantry and armored horsemen.

Ironically, the hussar battle dress is similar to the Turks' uniform; the urgency of war demands the most efficient gear for the task at hand. At the end of the

fifteenth century, after the hussars successfully drove the Turks back from the southern borders of Hungary, their social standing was dramatically improved. Hussar leaders were soon among the highest nobility, and the dashing hussar costume soon became an article of national dress, worn even by the most powerful men at court. In 1515 King Ulászló wore a hussar outfit at a gathering of his noblemen; in 1525 King Lajos II appeared before eleven thousand noblemen all clad in hussar uniforms.

In 1526 the Turks defeated the Magyars at Mohács in a battle in which Lajos II was killed. The marriage contract between Lajos and his Hapsburg bride, Maria, stipulated that Ferdinand I, the bride's brother, would inherit the Hungarian throne if Lajos died, as he did, without an heir. This suited the Hungarian nobility, who felt that Hapsburg support would be valuable against the Turks. However, the lesser nobility, distrusting foreigners, threw their support to János Zápolya, a wealthy landowner. In an ungainly political *pas de deux*, the country had two kings, the power of each limited by that of the other. Zápolya, despite his large army, could not get complete control of the country, and Ferdinand could not get enough aid from his brother Miksa, the Holy Roman Emperor, to put Zápolya down. János Zápolya died in 1541, leaving an infant son, János Sigismund. Zápolya's troops sided with the Turks, while Ferdinand took the reins of power in Buda Castle. Through a clever series of moves, the Turks took the castle without the Magyars realizing it had happened. Ultimately Ferdinand and Zápolya's followers settled their differences. Soon the southern part of the country was under Turkish rule, the western and northern borders with Austria had become part of the Hapsburg Empire, and Erdély (Transylvania) remained a separate state under János Sigismund. The country remained rent three ways for one hundred fifty years, challenged all the while by the Turks.

Many contemporary reports tell of the pomp and splendor that marked events at the Hungarian court in the sixteenth and seventeenth centuries. Perhaps the most picturesque account of these visually stunning spectacles is the one by the seventeenth-century historian Péter Apor:

> The lords wore crane-feathered fur caps, sabers with colored stones and pearls, and even decorated their horses with fringed gear. They wore velvet headdresses of expensive metals, sometimes with two crane feathers, along with silver stirrups and on their boots golden spurs laden with diamonds, rubies, and emeralds. Their servants wore eagle feathers, panther, tiger, or wolf skins, and large silver buttons. . . .

The main pieces comprising a civilian's costume were the dolman (jacket), the *mente* (outercoat), pants, boots, and a high fur cap. The shirt, first introduced in the Renaissance, was still an important item of clothing.

Men actually wore two shirts, one over the other. The one underneath was made of simple linen. The outer shirt was finer and decorated with openwork, metallic embroidery, and lace. The Hungarian-style shirt was loose fitting and had wide sleeves and a stand-up collar. It was adorned with cut-work embroidery at the wrists and collar. The finest shirts were flat embroidered in gold and silver. These were sewn by girls and given to their husbands as part of the trousseau. In 1561 one bride's trousseau contained forty such opulently decorated shirts. Only the most elaborate of these were given to the groom; the rest were passed out among the wedding guests.

The Hungarian-style hauberk was a padded silk or taffeta garment worn with armor, or as armor. In 1593 Gyorgy Thurzó wrote to his wife that he had been saved from injury by his taffeta shirt, although the shirt itself had been slightly damaged. Péter Apor tells us that during peacetime hauberks "made of some weak material . . . whose arms, chest, and collar were vividly embroidered" were worn by "young lads."

The quintessentially Hungarian item of men's clothing was the dolman. This flowing garment, open in the front, replaced the waistcoat after the Renaissance. The dolman reflects the mixture of eastern and western styles that were both influencing Hungarian fashion in the seventeenth century. The garment had the small, round, stand-up collar of the German-style shirt, but was otherwise cut like a caftan, open in the front and sometimes worn with the lapels overlapping. The sleeve — which has lent its name to the modern dolman sleeve — was part of the main pattern piece, with the side seam continuing along under the arm. The sleeve was worn short enough to reveal the elaborate embroidery on the shirt sleeves underneath (Fig. 49). Late in the seventeenth century the most popular style of dolman hung to mid-thigh and was worn mainly on holidays, at court, and during national festivals. The older ankle-length style was worn only on state visits to the Turkish sultan.

The *mente*, which was worn over the dolman, probably derived from the French *manteau* (coat). Péter Apor described this garment, a cross between the Renaissance coat and the eastern caftan: "The pompous *mente* was long with a large collar that hung down the middle of the back, covered half the arm, and hung over the chest. The two sleeves dangled to the ground. . . . Sometimes the sleeve material was stitched up so that it lay in folds over the arm." In the sixteenth century the *mente* reached the shins and could make walking a hazard unless a man tucked his "tails" into his belt. A shorter version, originally worn for riding, later came into general use.

The main ornamentation on all Hungarian clothes of the sixteenth and seventeenth centuries was silver and gold buttons, sometimes encrusted with precious stones. These were beautifully crafted by gold- and silversmiths and were often extravagant: Gábor Bethlen had two pairs of diamond buttons made up of 104 stones. Gold braid was used instead of buttonholes.

The form-fitting Hungarian pants were often made of broadcloth and were slit to the knee and held together with silver clasps. The Hungarian word for boot (*csizma*) is of Turkish origin. The most favored boots in Hungary were the knee-high variety in soft gray or yellow leather either imported from Turkey or copied by local craftsmen. A man also might wear a half-shoe that laced on the inside. Until the eighteenth century all shoes were reinforced or decorated with steel.

Men's hats were made of broadcloth trimmed with close-cropped fur. These tall caps were sometimes adorned with silver aigrettes and ostrich and eagle plumes.

The men's hairstyles of the seventeenth century were unusual — utterly unlike the French "lion"-type curls. Edouard Brown, an English doctor on a visit to Hungary in 1669–70, noted with surprise that the Magyars shaved their heads and left only a curly "forelock" like the Turks. Variations of the western hairstyle could also be found, but throughout the seventeenth century the bizarre Turkish style prevailed. Men wore a

*Fig. 51. The golden age of metalworking extended to saddlery. This example is of olive brown velvet embroidered in silver and set with turquoises and other stones. The bridle, breast strap, neck strap, and tail case are of leather covered with silver and brass plaques set with stones. Hungarian National Museum, Budapest. Photo: Joshua Greene.*

centuries wore what their contemporaries in Europe were wearing. The earlier Italian-, German-, and Spanish-influenced styles gave way to dresses modeled on the French baroque fashions. In the seventeenth century such things were imported from Vienna. In 1612 Gyorgy Thurzó had his aides buy the following items in Vienna for his daughter, Maria: gold material for dresses, with matching gold trimmings and linings; flowery silver material for a dress, with a thin gold lining; and livid velvet for a skirt with fur trimming. For a long dress flowery blue material with silver fur trimming and gold lining for sleeves was purchased. The list continued for pages.

Out of the German and later the Spanish Renaissance styles —with their laced waists enhanced by such Hungarian touches as lavish embroidery at the hems and the addition of lace-trimmed aprons—the Hungarian folk costume emerged (Fig. 50). This ensemble, worn on festive occasions and holidays, consisted of an amply frilled blouse, a laced bodice, an apron-overskirt, a *mente*, and a *párta* or chignon cover. The skirt came in two lengths: floor length, which was called "short," and a version with a long train. The skirt was sewn from solid-colored velvet or damask to set off the embroidery more effectively. Blue, dark red, and purple were the favorite colors, with silver or gold brocade for decoration.

The low-cut sleeveless boned corset was as amply decorated as the skirt. This was laced up the front with cord held in elaborately designed metal clasps. The apron was trimmed on three sides with a wide lace border. A Spanish-style cape was worn over the dress, although a woman also wore a shuba or a *mente* similar to the man's garment. A longer version of the *mente*, trimmed with fur and gathered at the waist, was worn by both men and women in the seventeenth century.

Young women wore *pártas* on their heads. These were decorated with enameled agrafes and pearls. An older woman wore a wider version of the *párta*, pushed farther back on the head. Only married women wore the headpiece of flat metal plates decorated with pearls.

When a woman dressed in western clothes she wore

twirled mustache with or without a beard. The Hungarian mustache was such a part of a man's visage that during the gymnastics exhibition organized by Prince Ferdinand in Austria in 1557, the Austrian nobility and even Ferdinand himself wore masks representing Hungarian facial features — and the ubiquitous mustache.

Hungarian women of the sixteenth and seventeenth

high-heeled bottines (short boots), but a woman in Hungarian costume wore metal-heeled shoes just as men did. A kerchief was carried in the hand; fans did not gain popularity in Hungary until the mid-seventeenth century.

The seventeenth century has been called the golden age of the goldsmith in Transylvania. Every woman wore pearls at her throat and diamond earrings. At her waist she wore a metal belt decorated with enamelwork and stone insets; necklaces and brooches were similarly decorated.

The Hungarians and Austrians coexisted for two centuries under an uneasy peace. Because they feared losing their independence—especially their freedom from taxation—the nobility asserted their right to choose a king who would support their policies. There were many confrontations between the frustrated nobles and the Austrian imperialist ruler before he swayed the noblemen to his position. Constant scuffles with the Turks had weakened the country, and the common people felt abandoned by the Austrian monarchy. The lesser nobility and the peasants, whose lands were being looted by the Austrians as well as the Turks, were in a state of revolt. First under the leadership of István Bocskay and Gábor Bethlen and later, in 1676, under Imre Thököly, the Transylvanian people withdrew and declared their right to self-government.

In 1683 the Hapsburgs defeated the Turks at Vienna, and the Treaty of Karlowitz was signed in 1699. The document brought peace, but divided Hungary into three parts and brought a wave of German-influenced reforms. The disappointed lower class turned to Ferenc Rákóczi, son of Imre Thököly and the heir to the Transylvanian throne. The insurgents, or "Kurucok" as they were called, mounted the revolution of 1703. The revolution was a failure, but the uniform of Ferenc's men, the old-fashioned dolman cropped very short, became the standard costume for men at court. This dashing uniform, in the *csákora* cut, was heavily decorated with passementerie. The applied decoration was not only beautiful, but helped protect the wearer from sword wounds. The spectacular-looking uniform that remained popular all over Europe and in London and

*Fig. 53. Man's gala costume of about 1790. Both the dolman and mente are shorter than those on the example from earlier in the century, and the entire costume has been elaborately embroidered. Hungarian Museum of Applied Arts, Budapest.*

Moscow until the outbreak of World War I evolved from the Hungarian hussar garb.

Rákóczi's defeated troops were dispersed throughout Europe. Some of the exiles formed the first foreign hussar regiment in France. Maria Theresa was so taken with the dashing hussars that she made them members of her best regiments.

Despite the failure of Rákóczi's freedom movement, the Szatmar Treaty was signed in 1711. It insured a degree of Hungarian independence. Relations with Austria were eased, and the aristocracy paid frequent visits to Maria Theresa's court. She chose her elite bodyguard from among the finest Hungarian aristocracy and dressed them in spectacular Kuroc outfits. She often dressed her heir, Joseph II, in the Hungarian national costume.

During the first half of the eighteenth century the dolman was worn cut close to the body and hemmed at mid-thigh. The *mente* too was closer cut, and on both garments the passementerie was finer than before. Fine gold and silver embroidery was also fashionable.

After midcentury French fashions began to filter into Hungary by way of Vienna—brought by foreign travelers—even protestant priests. One observer commented that the priests brought with them "wigs, underwear, watches, shoes with silver buckles ... and an occasional wench." The Hungarians found the French styles absurd. Even so, they eventually prevailed. Not everyone wore the French knee breeches, but the tricorne hat was seen everywhere. White powdered wigs became especially popular. Contemporary pictures show a ludicrous sight: Hungarian lords clad in their dolmans and *mentes*, with their twirled mustaches and chunky bodies, sporting full Rococo-style wigs. The hairpieces even became a requisite part of the military uniform.

Despite resistance from traditionalists, the European styles eventually flourished in Hungary. Not that the national costume diminished in popularity. There were two distinct types of dress: the traditional Hungarian one, which was undeniably influenced by the foreign styles, and Hungarian copies of European styles.

The suit of Samuel Teleki, a Transylvanian chancellor, was made in 1760–70 (Fig. 52). It faithfully depicts the shift toward European style in the Hungarian dress. The gray violet *csákora*-cut dolman was made of silk, reached the upper third of the thigh, and fit the body snugly. The fuller sleeve also shows the European influence, as does the knee-length mink-bordered *mente*. This garment resembles the French jerkin, not only in its length, but also in its contoured back, which is cut from three pieces of material and accented at the seams with soutache. In time fine embroidery in gold replaced soutache as decoration; eventually the thigh area of pants was decorated with embroidery — not soutache — at the side seams. The ankle boot, in gray leather lavishly decorated with golden embroidery, is a throwback to an earlier style.

Gradually the shape of the dolman evolved into a sleeveless waistcoat adorned with silk embroidery. By the end of the eighteenth century the *mente* was worn as a proper frockcoat, patterned after the European style. By the end of the century the *mente* was very short—almost like a hip-length spencer—open-fronted and often trimmed with fur. The dolman, the *mente*, and the pants were all decorated with elaborate floral designs embroidered in silk (Fig. 53).

Women's fashions changed little in the course of the eighteenth century. The traditional laced bodice and aproned costume remained in vogue for festivals, holidays, and balls. For everyday wear a woman chose her gowns from Paris or Vienna.

Péter Apor was a foe of these foreign fashions. He angrily maintained that at least the old Hungarian styles "did not make it seem like the breasts were being offered for market, as with the new styles." The sleeves on the new European white batiste blouses were less full and—a Hungarian touch—were tied together with three ribbons in several places (Fig. 54). Flat-stitched embroidery became popular during the 1770s and 80s; "needle painting" was used to apply naturalistic Rococo-style flowers — poppies, margueritas, and daisies — to the hems and waistbands of skirts (Fig. 55). In line with the European mode, the lacing of the bodice extended farther down onto the skirt in a square

shape. The silhouette of a woman's body was accentuated by whalebone stays or a corset of gold or silver mesh. In the last decade of the century the corset disappeared, and the bodice became shorter and rounder. Skirts became wider and were sometimes held out with hoops made of chicken wire.

By the end of the eighteenth and beginning of the nineteenth century the traditional gala Hungarian costume was worn less often. In the provinces a man wore the traditional dolman and *mente* only to political meetings. Otherwise the European fashions prevailed. In Buda and in Pest (they were not united until 1870) the only dolmans seen were worn by provincial visitors.

In 1830 Ferdinand V was crowned king of Hungary at Pozsony. During the events surrounding the coronation the fashions of the past century were revived. the brocaded silk-damask dolmans were the old-style, closely cut version worn mid-thigh length. The hem jutted out in *csákora* fashion, the collar was a narrow stand-up type, and rows of finely made string buttons decorated the front and the cuffs. A gold or silver cord belt was wrapped around the waist, and a beautifully decorated sword hung from it. A wide *mente* was worn *panyóka* fashion, slung from one shoulder. The front of the *mente* and the slit portions of the sleeves were closed with frogging. The backs of both the dolman and *mente* were cut from three pieces of fabric and decorated with soutache in a style reminiscent of the eighteenth century. The form-fitting silk pants had Brandenbourg frogs at the thighs.

Count Domokos Bethlen wore such an ensemble to Queen Victoria's coronation in 1838 (Fig. 56). The dolman is made of cranberry-colored velvet with gold and silver embroidery on it. The silver and gold buttons were adorned with pearls and almandines. The black velvet *mente* is embroidered much like the dolman. The large turned-back collar is trimmed with black fur. The beautiful leather boots are embroidered in gold with a grapeleaf design.

The women's dresses were variations on the Biedermeier style that had flourished in Vienna since 1814. The dresses retained the Hungarian flavor in their peaked bodices but displayed a daring décolleté (Fig.

Fig. 56. Gala costume worn by Count Domokos Bethlen to the coronation of Queen Victoria in 1838. Hungarian National Museum, Budapest.

Fig. 57. Portrait of Henrik Kugler, a well-known confectioner, and his family. About 1860. The women's dresses show the influence of the Viennese Biedermeier style in their décolletés and wide skirts. Hungarian National Museum, Budapest.

Fig. 58. Gala dress of the wife of Lord Chief Justice György Majláth. 1867–96. Bodice of dark red velvet trimmed with gold soutache. Neckline edged with gold lace. Skirt of white silk moiré embroidered with gold tinsel and trimmed with gold lace. Mente of dark red velvet trimmed with gold soutache and gold lace. Hungarian National Museum, Budapest. Photo: Joshua Greene.

57) and had wider, ruffled skirts supported by crinolines; the narrower waist was marked by a raised seam. The sleeves of the "Biedermeier"-style Hungarian gala dresses were tied with ribbons in several places, just as on women's dresses of the eighteenth century.

Socially and economically Hungary lagged behind the rest of Europe in the nineteenth century. Many Hungarian nationalist leaders felt that only by breaking away from Austria could their country assert herself and generate more trade and industry. In this political struggle, the national costume once again became a powerful symbol of political independence.

Hungary was not the only country to use clothing in this political way. Jacques-Louis David was designing classical-style clothes for his fellow Frenchmen. However, those garments had no true connection to French political history, whereas the dolman and *mente* actually were the traditional Hungarian costume. The black broadcloth dolman worn in Hungary in the 1840s surpassed the European frockcoat in popularity.

On March 15, 1848, revolution broke out in Pest. But within a year the uprising had been quelled, and its leaders had been either killed or expelled. The poet Sándor Petőfi died in the conflict; Lajos Kossuth fled to western Europe and America. Most of the rank-and-file rebels were jailed or hanged.

Naturally the defeat of the freedom movement affected the popularity of the traditional costume. These clothes were put away in the fifties, not to be seen again until about 1860, when folk dress made a comeback everywhere in Europe. Everyone on all levels of Hungarian society wore the traditional styles, and no one would be seen in public without soutache on his or her clothes.

In 1867 Austria and Hungary settled their differences, and one of the conditions of the truce was self-rule for Hungary. The most significant outcome of the treaty was the coronation of Franz Joseph I in Buda in 1867. It was the Hungarian social event of the century, and nobility from all over Europe attended the coronation. The only other occasion to warrant such a display was the celebration held in 1896 to mark the thousandth year of the Hungarian nation. By this time the tradi-

THE IMPERIAL STYLE

tional costume was synonymous with the idea of gala in Hungary. Every family had at least two gala outfits — a colorful one and a somber one for important funerals. People who had no heirloom gala clothes made them by copying costumes from paintings.

The most popular colors in the early nineteenth century were pale blue and clear red trimmed with gray or white fur. Later in the century purple, dark red, and deep gray were the colors of choice, with mink or marten trim. These sedate colors contrasted sharply with the vivid colors in vogue in Paris, London, and Vienna. The traditional dresses were decorated with jewelry based on eighteenth-century designs. The men's buttons, belts, *mente* sashes, swords, and aigrettes were lavishly enameled and inlaid with turquoise, coral, and other precious stones.

The most outstanding exhibition of women's gala costumes took place at the 1867 coronation and at the 1916 coronation of Karl I (Karoly IV of Hungary), the last Hapsburg monarch to rule Hungary. Women and girls of the aristocracy eagerly displayed the old family costumes passed down for generations. The European fashions were not ignored, but the new styles were made to incorporate facets of the old traditional dress.

Lord Chief Justice Majláth's wife owned a court dress of white moiré with a train nearly ten feet long and richly embroidered in gold (Fig. 58). The whalebone-reinforced bodice is of deep red velvet. The gold cord lacing is strung through clips made in the seventeenth century. The costume was worn three times: to the 1867 coronation of Franz Joseph I, in 1896, and to Karl I's coronation in 1916. On the last occasion it was worn by Mrs. Majláth's daughter.

After the 1870s Hungarian styles were not worn for everyday activities. The masses of crinolines that supported the gala dresses were a nuisance. Most women eagerly accepted the French styles that came to Hungary through Vienna. Budapest itself was an important fashion capital from which fashion trends were disseminated to eastern Europe and the Balkan countries, and the Hungarian dressmakers' and tailors' work was much in demand.

The golden age of Hungarian costume has passed, but echoes of it are still seen in riding habits and sporting clothes with hooked closures and in Hungarian-style embroidery of tulips and carnations. These details live in the fashions of today and continue the grand tradition of Hungarian costume.

Fig. 59. The parliament
buildings in Budapest, seen
from across the Danube.
The Bettmann Archive.

# A View of Hungary

By Paul Mathias, Former Chief Editor for America,
Paris-Match

The eighteenth century started late in Hungary—
very late indeed. In fact, by the year 1700 the major
part of the country had been under Turkish occupation
for nearly two centuries (Fig. 60). From the battle of
Mohács in 1526 and the fall of Buda to the defeat of
Suleiman the Magnificent before Vienna in 1683 and
the liberation of Buda in 1686, there was an endless war
going on.

The Hungarians had to give up the heart of their
country—all the lowlands—and defend themselves in
their castle-fortresses in Transylvania and the lower
reaches of the northern Carpathians.

When the country was finally totally liberated in 1699
by a coalition of European armies under the leadership
of Prince Eugene of Savoy, it lay in total shambles.
Whereas there had been twelve million Hungarians at
the beginning of the sixteenth century, there were a
mere two and a half million left at the beginning of the
eighteenth. And there was emptiness in the heart of the
country as it bled to death in the defense of Europe.

There were only three cities left: Kolozsvár, the capital of Transylvania, Kassa in the northern Carpathians,
and, on the western edge (near Vienna) the official capital, Pozsony, where parliament met. Buda was in ruins
and Pest nonexistent in 1700.

The eighteenth century bloomed in Hungary when
Maria Theresa became queen in 1740 (Fig. 61). Daughter of the last Hapsburg sovereign, Karl VI, she had
to fight for her succession and rights in four wars, the
last of which ended in 1763.

These endless wars asked for armies, and the Hungarians generously furnished men. They were the more
generous because they liked Maria Theresa, who
appealed to their gallantry.

The armies in turn needed to be furnished, not only
with arms and uniforms, but with an enormous amount
of food. Hungary was the granary of the empire, and in
half a century—between 1713 and 1763—the most
immense fortunes were made by the greatest Hungarian landowners: Koháry, Eszterházy, Pálffy, Grassalkovich, Széchenyi, Zichy, Batthyány, Károlyi,
Andrássy. They all had hundreds of thousands of acres
of rich land; the first two families had well over a million

acres each. They built not one, but several castles each,
and while they still spent a lot of their time in their
palaces in Vienna, they went more and more often to
their country estates, not only to hunt, but also to live.

Viennese elegance, which was influenced by French
elegance, met and mingled with the old Hungarian
country way of life, which had its special style: there
was driving in carriages, riding day in and day out,
hunting, shooting, sporting.

There were really two sorts of country life in Hungary: the one enjoyed by the immensely rich and powerful—not more than twenty families—and the one led
by the wealthy landed gentry, the backbone of the nation until the rise of the bourgeoisie in the second half
of the nineteenth century.

The immensely rich were often extravagant. When
Maria Theresa came to visit Prince Grassalkovich in the
summer of 1763, the prince, knowing that the queen
liked snow and driving in sleighs, decided to bluff her.
For eighteen months he had all the salt mined in his
numerous and immense salt mines in northern Hungary shipped down the Danube to the township of Pest
twelve miles from his castle at Gödöllő. When the
queen arrived in the summer heat at the river landing
at Pest, she found a jewel-studded silver sleigh filled
with the rarest fur robes and the road to Grassalkovich's
castle paved a foot high with snow-white salt. She
mounted the sleigh, and, driven by the prince and six
galloping white horses, arrived at the castle fifty min-
utes later, hot in the ninety-five-degree heat, sneezing
from powdery salt, and wondering what would happen
next.

Maria Theresa never forgot this episode. When
Grassalkovich was ruined by his wild extravagances a
few years later and was dying as a pauper, she sent him a
present and a message saying that she would always
remember their sleigh ride. He didn't ask for more.

Between 1762 and 1767 the Eszterházys built the castle that will always carry their name. Another "Versailles," as the French ambassador called it, it had 140
rooms, a theater, and a chapel, four hundred servants
(three to a room), custom-made service of Meissen
seven thousand pieces strong, a private orchestra, a

Fig. 60. Hungarians paying homage to the Turks. Engraving, by Romeyn de Hooghe, from Leopoldi...nec non Johannis III acta prope obsessam a turc tart Reb. etc. Viennam Austriae, *published in Amsterdam by Nicolas Visscher, 1683. The Metropolitan Museum of Art, New York. Elisha Whittelsey Fund, 1949. 49.95.741 (2).*

Fig. 61. Empress Maria Theresa in her Hungarian coronation gown. Oil on canvas, about 1740, school of Marten von Meytens. Kunsthistorisches Museum, Vienna. Inv. no. 3458.

apud N. Visscher cum Privil

THE IMPERIAL STYLE

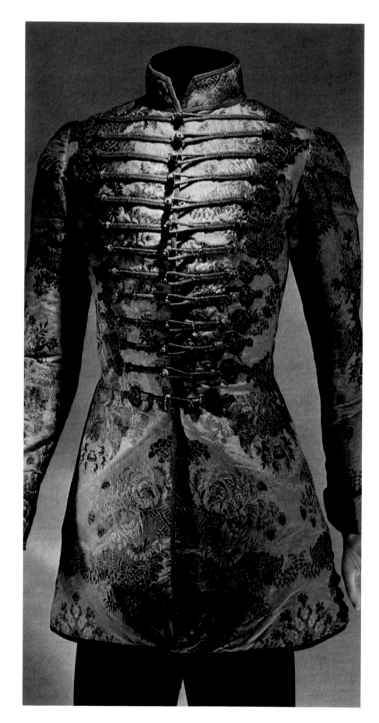

private troop of actors, and always performances by the greatest musicians—from Haydn to Beethoven.

It was naturally easy to have hundreds of servants at that time. Thousands of peasants worked the Eszterházy lands, and they in turn were proud to see their daughters and sons garbed in pompous livery, working in the castle, serving the prince.

Prince Eszterházy and his princess dressed exactly like their equals in Versailles or Schönbrunn. Only when they went to court in Vienna, or to parliament at Pozsony did they put on their magnificent national costumes covered with jewels from the plumes of the hats, to the spurs of their boots (Fig. 62).

In parliament Latin was spoken as late as 1832. At home the nobles spoke French, Hungarian, and German, not always in that order, and often mixing them up. They ate a lot, drank a lot, and gambled a lot, and kept the family fortune intact by keeping it in one hand—that of the head of the family.

Many poor cousins married into the rich landed gentry and formed the bridge between the very few very rich and the solid backbone of more or less wealthy landed gentry. The landed gentry lived a more leisurely life than the nobles. Because they did not have to go to court, they had more time for sport and intellectual pursuits. They read more, and, at the end of the eighteenth century, they gave the country its first poets and writers.

Their castles were smaller, they dressed more simply, yet each of them had his *diszmagyar*, a jewel-studded gala costume, tucked away and worn rarely, but always ready for another appearance—a coronation or a marriage (Fig. 63).

The emperor or empress of Austria was also the king or queen of Hungary. Maria Theresa's son Joseph II did not want to be crowned with the crown of St. Stephen of Hungary, as he did not want to take the oath on the kingdom's constitution. Every Hungarian called him "the king in a hat" (Fig. 64). He died in 1790, and his brother Leopold succeeded him. He took the oath and was crowned king.

Slowly Buda and Pest were growing, and some of the rich who had a palace in Vienna and two or three castles

THE IMPERIAL STYLE

Fig. 63. "Hungarians," from
a series of wedding cos-
tumes. English stipple
engraving colored by hand,
about 1810. The Metropolitan Museum of Art, New
York. Harris Brisbane Dick
Fund, 1948. 48.90.11.

Fig. 64. "The king in a hat,"
Joseph II, with coronation
insignia. Oil on canvas,
about 1780. Kunsthistorisches Museum, Vienna. Inv.
no. 7472.

HUNGARIANS.

THE IMPERIAL STYLE

*Fig. 65. Buda Castle.
The Bettmann Archive.*

*Fig. 66. Elegance is a
timeless quality among
Hungarian women.
Photograph, about 1900,
by F. Berkeley Smith.*

in the country finally decided to build "something" in Buda (or later Pest). These were more houses than palaces, but, when, after the French Revolution, Napoleon started to "visit" Vienna, it came in handy to have a house in Buda-Pest.

From 1790 on, the king named a cousin, an archduke, to reside in the royal castle of Buda (Fig. 65). Thus a new sociopolitical center was created, and slowly the center of social life moved away from Pozsony toward the center of the country.

Hungarians were still galloping, hunting, shooting, and planting trees in the enormous English-style parks around their castles. The Napoleonic Wars were just over, but the armies were gone and Europe seemed smaller; ideas traveled quicker.

It was then that István (Steven) Count Széchenyi, whom his countrymen later called "the greatest Hungarian," appeared. He was brilliant, elegant, liberal—an innovator. He built the first chain bridge between Buda and Pest to create not only a capital city, but a grand center of elegance. He organized the first horseraces in Hungary, and sold to his countrymen, and women, the idea that it was stylish and elegant to work for the nation, for people, for progress.

Born in 1792, elected to parliament in 1825, he was married to the supremely elegant Countess Clam-Gallas. He made several trips to England and brought back to his country ideas and style with an English flavor.

The portraits, miniatures, and watercolors of beautiful Hungarian ladies of the period show them to be a little Biedermeier, very romantico-Hungarian, with a somehow English touch. Maybe it is their beautiful skin, very like the English complexion. And there is a touch of somber elegance in their bearing and the way they hold their heads (Fig. 66).

The post-Napoleonic years show us not only the first portraits of the city and small-town bourgeoisie, but also country scenes in which folk elements figure strongly. One sees scenes of shepherds standing near their flocks, in lovely "shubas" down to their feet. The country women are shown dressed in colored, many-layered skirts—to just below the knee—presenting a

Fig. 67. Transylvanian
peasants in traditional
costume. Engraving, early
twentieth century. Photo:
The Bettmann Archive.

Fig. 68. Lajos Kossuth.
Engraving, late nineteenth
century, by J. C. Buttre.
Photo: The Bettmann
Archive.

*Engraved by J.C.Buttre*

*L. Kossuth*

GOVERNOR OF HUNGARY.

AUBURN, N.Y.
Derby & Miller

slightly idealized image of peasant life (Fig. 67).

The ideas of the 1830s and 40s—the liberal breeze of Széchenyi and Deák—soon brought along Lajos Kossuth, a charismatic, nationalistic leader (Fig. 68).

In 1848, as the breeze turned into a storm all over Europe, the Hungarians again had to choose how far not to go. After nearly a century and a half, they were now more or less at peace with the Hapsburgs.

But the Hapsburgs were running an empire—the first united Europe, say some—and constantly forgot to take into account the nationalism of the Hungarians. Soon the lovely ladies were tearing up their gauze and clothes, setting up hospitals, and nursing the dying young men who fought the army of the new emperor—eighteen-year-old Franz Joseph I.

He was not crowned king of Hungary in 1848; he did not want to take the oath. The princes and counts and their ladies had no chance to wear their beautiful gala costumes. There was no coronation, no ball.

After more than a year of first victorious battles and then defeat before the united armies of the emperor and the czar, the Hungarians had to put away their costumes and jewels for nearly a generation of silence and mourning.

Then came 1867, and the emperor, after being defeated by the Prussians, suddenly remembered that he was also king of Hungary. With his beautiful Empress Elisabeth he came to Budapest, and out of nowhere the costumes of pomp and beauty appeared when the imperial couple were crowned king and queen of Hungary (Fig.69). But Elisabeth was much more than a queen to the Hungarians. Her beauty and elegance and restlessly romantic nature found an immediate echo among Hungarians of all sorts. Not only the aristocracy, the landed gentry, and the new bourgeoisie, but the simple folk themselves soon cherished her image. Thousands of prints of the queen were sold and hung on the walls of castles, houses, and huts (Fig. 70). And Elisabeth responded fully. She loved Hungarians and was surrounded by them.

For more than thirty years she galloped and jumped and hunted across the fields and forests and hills of Hungary. It was a true love story between a nation and a

THE IMPERIAL STYLE

woman, and when, in 1896, she came to Budapest for the thousandth anniversary of the Hungarian nation, the fifty-nine-year-old, sad and beautiful queen could really call it a homecoming.

For Hungary it was a year of glitter and splendor; for Elisabeth it was a year of farewell. On September 10, 1898, she was stabbed to death by a mad anarchist on the shores of Lake Geneva. Her last words were: "At last." In Hungary the grief and shock were total. The simple dress she wore when she died is still in the National Museum at Budapest.

Then suddenly the twentieth century arrived. Budapest grew into one of the great capitals of Europe. "Hungarian chic" and "Hungarian style" became catch phrases in Europe in the years before 1914. But chic and style can be acquired; elegance cannot. The elegance of the Hungarians is inborne and has remained intact throughout their long history of sorrow and splendor.

# Viennese Men's Fashions

By Dora Heinz, Former Curator of the Textile Collection, Austrian Museum of Applied Arts, Vienna

In November 1786 a pamphlet called "Project for a New Dress Regulation to Be Observed This Coming Year in Vienna" was published. The anonymous author decried the fact that anyone could dress as luxuriously as his means allowed and lamented the outrages that could result: a member of the aristocracy could be addressed by a craftsman with the familiar "thou" — or even less respectfully — simply because his coat was of simple cloth, or, as happened not infrequently, hair-dressers and servants could be greeted politely in stores and other public places and even given preferential treatment just because they were dressed in the latest fashions. The unknown writer proposed subtle regulations of dress that would make it possible to recognize a man's trade or quality of birth by the way he dressed; these rules would be enforced by a "dress police." Despite the author's emotional tone, one important fact is clear: the privilege of the upper classes to distinguish themselves by their dress had been abandoned in Vienna well before the time of the French Revolution. In that conflict the right to wear special clothing was bloodily wrested from the aristocracy.

In spite of the anonymous Viennese author's zeal, no dress regulation was enforced in Vienna at the end of the eighteenth century. The Viennese expressed their freedom in the way they dressed. In 1799 an essay titled "Bernadotte to the Gentlemen with the Wild Hair and Beards in Vienna" presented an imaginary diatribe by the French ambassador general Bernadotte to the men of Vienna who sported "wild hair and chops" without being of a republican conviction. The men who a few years later wore coats of "Napoleon green" despite their adamant hatred of Napoleon must have been similarly indifferent to the underlying political significance of their clothes.

An inconsistency in the way men dressed persisted in Vienna into the nineteenth century. Traditional fashions were worn with modern things as well as with items borrowed from the costumes of other countries. Every outrageous new development was mocked by local wags or satirized in essays like the 1803 "Letters of an Eipeldauer" written by the Viennese journalist Josef Richter, who maintained that in Vienna "the trousers are Turkish, the boots Prussian, the vest Hungarian, the waistcoat English and the hat Russian."

Although English fashion had strongly influenced men's styles in Vienna even before the turn of the century, the journals and almanacs published in Vienna illustrated Paris fashions exclusively, even when there was nothing new to report from Paris. The following description appeared beneath a fashion plate published in an issue of the Wiener Moden Journal of 1805: "The young gentlemen have not changed their costume, and there is nothing to remark except that triple vests have been discarded." The same journal, however, ran an article about "luxury" in which it was asserted that luxury is a necessary and desirable part of everyone's life and not to be reserved for the wealthy:

> We have seen a terrible example of what happens to a nation where luxury is repressed. When the Parisians affected republican simplicity in fashion during the Reign of Terror and at the beginning of the rule of the Directoire all trade and craftsmanship ceased, all factories and workshops shut down, and a famine threatened. ... Only the production of luxuries insures wealth, volume of trade, welfare, and their beautiful consequences: education and morality for every class; without luxury the population would be decimated or exist only in poverty, deprivation, and crudity.

It should be understood that the author of the article was not advocating unbounded luxury or wasteful spending. He was proposing a plan — expressed here through fashion — to increase trade and to free his country from dependence on imported luxury goods. Both Maria Theresa and Joseph II had earlier spared no effort or expense to subsidize the Austrian fashion industry. Through their efforts the foundations for an independent industry were laid, but their plans did not reach fruition until the beginning of the nineteenth century. The rise of Viennese fashion coincided with the Congress of Vienna.

The congress was of course not the cause of the international popularity of and the general acclaim for the Viennese styles, but it was an excellent occasion for testing and proving the sense of style that had been developing since the middle of the eighteenth century.

The Viennese gentlemen chose their clothes with an assured sense of what suited them best from among the many possibilities available. They never stepped outside the mainstream of the international development of men's fashion, which was dominated by the English, but they adopted the western European fashions in a way that was practical and suited their temper as well as their customs. It required great skill to create a simple line, such as that of trousers that fit "like marble." The Viennese tailors had to prove themselves to the demanding international clientele who participated in the congress. After all, these clothes underlined the figure and made every flaw obvious. The Viennese tailors, under pressure to perform quickly and to flatter this most discerning public, were overworked but were also given the incentive to attempt their best.

The Viennese always eschewed the "German national costume" in favor of more moderate continental fashions. Historical costumes or those resembling national costumes had always been popular for fancy-dress balls, but never for daily use. One of the highlights of the congress was the famous "Carousell" of November 23, 1814, at which not only the ladies, but also twenty-four "knights" were dressed in beautiful historical costumes of heavily embroidered velvets and silks. Equally successful was the costume ball given by the British envoy Sir Henry Wellesley in 1826, at which fantastic historical costumes were worn "under a romantic enchanted light" (Fig. 71). But in clothes for daily wear men wanted to be contemporary and European. It seems incredibly modern of a Viennese journalist of the time to have said that " any hint of European character, be it in habit or costume, should be recognized gratefully and encouraged."

During the Revolution the French had turned against everything that suggested the upper classes: powdered wigs, braids, precious silks and laces, culottes, silk stockings, and buckle shoes. One group of revolutionaries was even known by the name "sans-culottes" because of its ostentatious wearing of long trousers, the so-called pantalons. If one understands that clothing had enormous political significance in the nineteenth century, one can easily believe that an entire day of deliberation at the congress was devoted to the question of whether or not the Holy Alliance could recognize the pantalon or whether the culotte should be retained. Everyone acknowledged that the time for dress codes was over, so that no actual regulation was passed, but a compromise was accepted: for gala occasions court dress with culottes, silk stockings, and buckle shoes was obligatory, but pantalons could not be prohibited for daily wear. Most contemporary portraits — even political cartoons (Fig. 72) — show the participants in the traditional culottes. For a time tight, calf-length pantalons were accepted as ball dress, but by 1820 pantalons had become standard streetwear.

Immediately after the congress, when the Viennese fashion industry had passed its crucial test and a distinctive Viennese style had been launched, the first local fashion journal — the *Wiener Modenzeitung*, began publication. Its fashion plates were representations of clothes actually worn in the city. The illustrations enjoyed great popularity and were frequently imitated because they were beautifully drawn and well printed. Many of the originals were drawn by Johann Ender; the later plates were often drawn by Philipp von Stubenrauch and etched by Franz Stöber (Fig. 73).

The Viennese style in men's fashion had been established by 1820 and did not change significantly until the middle of the century. This simple, bourgeois fashion was worn by the nobility and the middle class alike, and even Emperor Franz I and members of the imperial family were seen in coats of plain cloth (Fig. 74). In 1813 the Swiss banker Jean Gabriel Eynard had remarked that "no one seems less like a sovereign and more like a bourgeois from a small provincial town" than Franz I. It was certainly partly his simple bourgeois appearance, along with his often rustic and witty ways, that made this emperor so particularly popular. His role model, Joseph II, had always worn unobtrusive dress for traveling incognito, but for Franz I it was a matter of course to dress simply for everyday.

The pride of the Viennese tailors was the tasteful and imaginative detail of their designs. The main articles of clothing — the waistcoat or redingote, trousers that

LE CONGRÈS.

were kept taut by straps run under the insteps, the vest or gilet, and, finally, the shirt with its stiff collar and the neckerchief or cravat—were common to men's fashions of all European countries. After dark fabrics came into use for coats and solid lighter colors for trousers, the expensive, patterned silks were dropped. Only the gilets and cravats, artistically knotted, remained as special colorful accents. Viennese silk weavers produced the richly ornamented fabrics for the gilets; rich velvets —especially voided velvets with small patterns—were also used. The gilets presented a great opportunity for embroiderers. A white piqué gilet was usually worn under a colorful one, which was adorned with jeweled buttons and a watch chain draped across the front. It

was not unusual for a well-to-do gentleman to own fifty gilets. Joseph Gunkel, Vienna's most renowned tailor, employed thirty assistants just to create gilets.

Gunkel, whose designs were often illustrated as the fashion plates in the *Wiener Modenzeitung*, gave his creations originality by the clever use of color and decoration. Passementerie played an important role in this. Gunkel's greatcoats recalled the embroidered rural costumes of the Balkans; some of his coats bore colorful braid ornament or double rows of buttons; others had closings that imitated braid. With these garments, which Gunkel gave such titles as "à la Cosak," he catered to the contemporary interest in oriental forms and patterns. His "fantasie coats" with wide,

THE IMPERIAL STYLE

Fig. 73. Two designs by
Joseph Gunkel. Fashion
plate in the Wiener
Zeitschrift für Kunst,
Literatur und Mode of
December 12, 1839. Drawn
by Johann Ender. Etched
by Franz Stöber. Museen
der Stadt Wien. Inv. no.
56.740/405.

loose cuts and rich decorations were not favorably
received, but housecoats made of cloth woven with
eastern motifs became the rage. A gentleman could
entertain at home in a "Turkish" morning coat, pantouf-
fles, and little cap (Fig. 75). The colorful oriental fabrics
were abundant in Vienna because of its lively trade with
the East.

The technical innovations of the early nineteenth
century had a profound effect on the production of fashion in Vienna. In 1839 the Viennese tailor Joseph Ritzenthaler published a "Thorough Representation of
Menswear Patterns after an Explantion of Line Drawing and the Use of the Doctrine of Proportions," the
first textbook explaining how to make and use propor-
tioned patterns for sewing. Ritzenthaler's system revo-
lutionized tailoring, which had previously relied on the
use of stencils. The next step, which was to include patterns in the fashion journals, was taken by the
*Nationalmodenzeitung* in 1848.

The invention Johann Nepomuk Reithoffer had
made in 1828 was no less significant than patternmak-
ing. Reithoffer devised a method of encasing rubber in
cotton thread to create elastic threads and fabrics.
These were marketed under the name "Federharz" and
immediately became indispensable in the fashion
industry. Reithoffer developed the first water-resistant
fabrics a short time later.

The sewing machine did not make an impact on Viennese fashion until well into the second half of the nineteenth century. Joseph Madersberger, a Tirolean jour-
neyman tailor, had built a machine in 1808, but it could
only produce straight seams. Even after the original
design was improved, Viennese tailors were slow to
accept the machine. Many tailors feared a loss of business if everything was made by the speedy machine.
Until well into the second half of the nineteenth century the best and most expensive Viennese tailors
proudly advertised that their suits and coats were all
hand sewn. "Handmade" was still the symbol of highest
quality.

In 1848, a year of great political tension, the political
significance of fashion once more became important.
The conflict between the culotte and the pantalon was

Wiener Moden.

Fig. 74. Portrait of
Emperor Franz I and his
family in a summerhouse.
Oil on canvas, 1826.
Museen der Stadt Wien.

THE IMPERIAL STYLE

recalled in an 1845 fashion article predicting that pants would soon be worn without straps: "Only a few more months and we will be set free; a free, unbridled pantalon will flap about our legs.... Long live the liberated pantalon! Anyone still in culottes cannot, of course, partake of this liberation." In the year of the revolution a caricature of Prince Klemens von Metternich showed him in white culottes, stockings, and buckled shoes, calling to his servant, "Bring me another pair of pants." The top hat — once the headgear of a progressive thinker—was now the property of the opposite faction. In 1848 the revolutionaries wore soft hats with wide brims, called "Kalabreser" or "Carbonari" hats; the top hat was nicknamed "Angströhre" ("chimney of fear"), since many wore it to avoid being suspected of harboring revolutionary sentiments.

The revolution of 1848 marked the end of a stage in Viennese men's fashion that had begun with the Congress of Vienna in 1814. The *Wiener Zeitschrift für Kunst, Literatur, Theater und Mode* appeared for the last time in 1848, and in 1859-60 the *Wiener Theater Zeitung*, which had published Parisian fashion designs, also ceased publication. During the second half of the nineteenth century originality was supressed more and more (Fig. 76). With the advent of the "suit" at the end of the 1860s, the possibility for colorful or contrasting combinations of coats and pants or for richly ornamented gilets was eliminated. Very soon the tie was the only aspect of the wardrobe with which to express individuality.

Many people complained of the monotony of men's fashions, yet no new styles emerged to counter the trend toward dullness. Only a few individual artists opposed the international dictatorship of fashion. The elaborate historical costumes worn at Hans Makart's renowned fetes—even those worn at the artist's grand parade in 1879 to celebrate the silver wedding anniversary of Emperor Franz Joseph I and Empress Elisabeth — had absolutely no influence on the forms of men's fashion.

The character of the men's tailoring trade in Vienna during the second half of the nineteenth century is marked by the competition between independent tai-

lors and the mass-produced clothing industry. The more popular the ready-made clothes became with the general populace, the more exclusive the tailor-made work became. Immaculate fabrics and first-class workmanship continued to distinguish the most elegant men's fashions. The quality and prices were so high that they insured exclusiveness. In a poll taken in 1896-97, only seven or eight gentlemen's tailors were registered

*Fig. 76. Fashion plate
in an issue of the* Wiener
Zcitschrift für Kunst,
Literatur und Mode *of
June 1862. Museen der
Stadt Wien. Inv. no.
84.290/4.*

for a population of about two million. The "ateliers" of
these tailors were located in the center of the city, and
there was usually a stock of fine fabrics adjacent to the
workshop. The leading tailors employed only the best
craftsmen, usually master tailors who worked at home.
It was necessary to be a regular customer of one of these
tailors if one were to be a respected member of the
upper class, and every apprentice tailor aspired to be
employed in one of the top establishments. Prices and
salaries varied considerably. The prices demanded by
one of the gentlemen's tailors, and, accordingly, the
salaries of his employees, were five to six times what
was asked in the suburbs. These few entrepreneurs,
who among themselves determined the elegant men's
fashion, continued the tradition Joseph Gunkel had
represented in the 1830s.

Certain tailors operated clothes-lending enterprises
and "abonnement" tailors' shops in addition to their
regular tailoring businesses. Here a gentleman could
contract to return used clothing in exchange for
entirely new pieces modestly priced. The secondhand
clothing trade was of course not operated by the tailors
of the upper classes. It was the beginning of the concept
of ready-made clothing and marked the advent of sizes
designated by numbers. More and more journeymen
tailors came into the employ of the large entrepreneurs, who, under the freedom of trade law passed in
1859, were not even required to have learned the
tailoring trade. A diffuse system of piece work done at
home grew and encouraged specialization. The inade-
quate training of apprentices raised sharp criticism,
and many efforts were made to raise the technical level
of tailoring in Vienna. In 1891 a union trade school was
founded to teach and preserve tailoring skills, and a so-
called Tailor's Academy followed in 1907, but the heyday of men's fashion in Vienna was at an end. An
attempt had been made to promote Viennese men's
fashions at the World Exhibition held in Vienna in 1873,
but English styles had dominated the event. When the
Austrian Museum for Art and Industry mounted a show
of Viennese fashion in the winter of 1915-16, it was devoted entirely to designs for women. Only a few fault-
less pieces of menswear were shown as a supplement.

*Fig. 77. Military flag of Austria-Hungary, 1867–1918. Museum of Military History, Vienna.*

*The black, crowned, double-headed eagle on a gold ground is the symbol of the Holy Roman Empire. The Holy Roman Emperors considered the use of the eagle in their heraldry a symbolic tie with the emperors of Rome. Although the eagle with two heads was used by the Russian czars to symbolize the eastern*

*orthodox church, the motif also symbolized Catholicism. The crest in the center of the eagle's body bears the colors of Austria: red-white (silver)-red. At the left is the Hapsburg lion; on the right are the larks of Lorraine.*

*Below the central crest hang the stars of the orders of Leopold (left) and the Iron Crown (right) and (below them) St. Stephen of Hungary. The star of the military order of Maria*

*Theresa hangs on a red and white sash. Below this the chain of the Order of the Golden Fleece appears.*

*Surrounding the central crest are the smaller crests of the kingdoms, duchies, and counties of the Hapsburg Empire. Counter-clockwise from the upper left, they are: Kingdom of Hungary; Kingdom of Lombardo-Venetia; Kingdom of Illyria (a division of the Napoleonic*

*Empire that once included Carinthia, Carniola, Gorizia, Istria, parts of Croatia, Dalmatia, Ragusa, and the Ionian Islands); Archduchy of Transylvania; County of Moravia and Duchy of Silesia; Princely county of Tirol; Duchies of Styria and Carinthia; Duchy of Salzburg; Archduchy of Lower Austria; Kingdom of Galicia; Kingdom of Bohemia.*

# Viennese Court Dress

By Georg J. Kugler, Curator of the Monturdepot and the Wagenburg, Kunsthistorisches Museum, Vienna

The following essay is a supplement to the article on Viennese men's fashions (pages 101–107), with remarks on court dress, court uniforms, and the livery of the servants of the imperial court of Vienna. The commentary pertains to the objects from the Monturdepot of the Hofburg in Vienna, many of which were shown publicly for the first time in the exhibition *Fashions of the Hapsburg Era: Austria-Hungary.*

The Monturdepot is still a storeroom; only a small selection of its contents is on display in Vienna. The vestments of the orders are shown in the Weltliche Schatzkammer (Imperial Treasure Chamber), and some of the liveries are on display in the Wagenburg (Carriage Collection) at Schönbrunn Palace. The collection of costumes stored in the Monturdepot was formed from the stock of liveries and uniforms left behind when the Austro-Hungarian Empire collapsed in 1918 and from the vestments of the knights of the orders of Austria. When the Monturdepot became part of the collections of the Kunsthistorisches Museum, many other pieces were purchased, and the collection was enlarged and enhanced significantly.

For a better understanding of Viennese court dress, one must know the cultural history of the imperial court of Vienna. The city had been the residence of the Hapsburg sovereigns since the fourteenth century; the Holy Roman Emperors had been Hapsburgs from the sixteenth to the end of the eighteenth century, when the French Revolution of 1789 and the subsequent rise and reign of Napoleon brought about the end of the era. The burden of three wars against revolutionary France had lain on the shoulders of Austria and Prussia, and Vienna, as the capital and residence of the head of the Holy Roman Empire of German Nations, had carried the responsibility for the struggle. But the cause was lost; the empire was conquered by Napoleon and totally reorganized. Parts of it were annexed to France; other parts were put under the protectorate of the Great Corse. Franz II, who had been reigning since 1792, dissolved the Holy Roman Empire in 1806 and became Austrian Emperor Franz I. After Napoleon's fall in 1815 the German principalities that had been under his protection became independent states.

Austria, which had been the largest state in the Holy Roman Empire, was, aside from Russia, the largest nation in Europe. After the Napoleonic catastrophe, Austria, under the guidance of Prince Klemens von Metternich, assumed the task of reorganizing Europe at the Congress of Vienna (1814–15), an event that was a turning point in European history (Fig. 78).

The Viennese court was known as the protector of tradition; its opponents considered it the rampart of reaction. The attitude in Paris after 1815 was rather ambivalent about the Revolution and the First Empire, with feelings vacillating between admiration and antipathy for both. In Vienna everyone feared and abhorred the political developments that had taken place in France after 1789 and wanted to erase even the memory of them. The Austrian Empire upheld the traditions of the Holy Roman Empire: the emperor kept the imperial black eagle on a gold ground as part of his crest (Fig. 77); the court charges were continued; the administration of the imperial household, the state, and the military continued along the traditional lines. After decades of war every aspect of life was influenced by the military, and everyone in public life wore a uniform. In an 1809 issue of *Journal des Luxus und der Moden,* published in Weimar, the Vienna correspondent reported: "The new fashions cannot win the gentlemen, since tasteful and rich uniforms are worn in all public offices."

This was absolutely true for the imperial court. Everything fashionable that could be associated in any way with revolutionary ideas was completely rejected despite the efforts of fashion journals like the *Wiener Modenzeitung* and others to popularize the fashions of the revolution. Free-flowing hair and a soft felt hat were symbols of "Jacobean" convictions. A popular expression in Vienna in 1799 held that unpowdered hair and a beard meant the same thing as a red, white, and blue cockade, the symbol of the French Revolution. But the court rejected just as strenuously the movement for a German national dress, which started about 1813 in Germany and found a strong supporter in the Viennese intellectual Caroline Pichler. The only approved court fashions were the gala dress and the robes of state of the ancient régime — the *habit à la française*.

The theatrical glamour of the Napoleonic Empire and the ostentatiousness of the costumes introduced by parvenus did have a certain effect on the clothes worn at the court of Vienna, but on the whole court dress did not change after the second half of the eighteenth century. The men's dress was of a decided military flavor; the role of the uniform was more important throughout the nineteenth century in Austria than anywhere else during peacetime (Fig. 79). Emperor Franz Joseph I (reigned 1848–1916) wore uniforms for almost every occasion and ordered all the archdukes and officers down to the youngest lieutenant to do the same.

In Austria, as elsewhere in Europe, a soldier's gear developed gradually into a military uniform at the beginning of the eighteenth century. It evolved not according to the continuous developments in fashion, but only from one dress regulation to the next. During the early years of the eighteenth century the dress of the aristocratic dignitaries and court officials developed into liveries. These too developed quite independently of fashion trends and were conceived to fulfill a yearning for ostentation and glamour on the part of individual princes. The old court dress was itself a " uniform" inasmuch as everyone wore it, but it was gradually replaced by the military uniform.

The only known portraits of Emperor Karl VI (king of Spain in 1703–1711, Holy Roman Emperor 1711–1740) show him dressed in his coronation vestments, the "Spanish" court dress, consisting of coat and culottes of gold brocade (Fig. 80), or the black Spanish national costume or hunting dress. His son-in-law Duke Franz Stephan of Lorraine, husband of Maria Theresa, was made Archduke of Tuscany in 1739 and Holy Roman Emperor in 1745. In portraits of the 1740s he is shown in the Rococo splendor of court dress — a red waistcoat and breeches embroidered in gold. Later portraits show him in a white uniform with red trim and lapels that indicate his infantry regiment. Military uniforms did not become acceptable at court until about 1750, and even then they were not universally worn because they were not compatible with the Spanish-Bur-

*Fig. 78. Emperor Franz I entering Vienna upon his return from Paris in 1814. Behind the emperor are officers of his archers body guard. Detail of a wall painting, by Peter Krafft. Hofburg, Vienna. Photo: Meyer, Vienna.*

THE IMPERIAL STYLE

Fig. 79. Garden banquet
at Schönbrunn Palace. Oil
on canvas, 1858, by
Siegmund l'Allemand.
Schönbrunn Palace,
Vienna. Photo: Meyer,
Vienna.

*Fig. 80. Emperor Karl VI in the Spanish court costume of gold brocade. On his chest he wears the diamanté of the Order of the Golden Fleece. Oil on canvas, about 1730, by Johann Gottfried Auerbach. Schönbrunn Palace, Vienna. Inv. no. 1810.*

gundian court etiquette.

It is interesting that Crown Prince Joseph (born 1741), eldest son of Franz Stephan and Maria Theresa, did not start wearing the uniform of the regiment of dragoons he headed until long after his younger brothers were in uniform. In a group portrait in Schönbrunn Palace painted in about 1751–52 (Fig. 81), Joseph stands between his brothers Carl Joseph (born 1745) and Peter Leopold (born 1747). Both brothers wear their uniforms, but Joseph is shown in gold-embroidered court dress. Archduke Carl Joseph (right) headed a Hungarian regiment for political reasons; all the other young archdukes, including Peter Leopold, were with the dragoons, traditionally regarded as the most distinguished branch of the armed forces. Carl Joseph's uniform has all the characteristics of Hungarian national dress. It consists of a white waistcoat with gold trim, blue and gold trousers, a coat of Hungarian cut, a dolman instead of a vest, long embroidered hose, and short yellow boots. It was only when Joseph was older that he had some influence in the question of dress. He had by then found his role model in Friedrich II, king of Prussia (reigned 1740–86), and after his accession as Holy Roman Emperor in 1765 he was always portrayed in his green light cavalry uniform (Fig. 82).

In their official state portraits the Austrian rulers were shown in uniform, in the vestment of the Order of the Golden Fleece (Fig. 83), or in coronation robes. The styles set by the sovereigns were reflected in the clothes of the high-ranking officers of the court, aristocratic society, and by the court servants of various ranks.

All the distinguished offices of the court were held by members of the aristocracy. They wore the uniforms of their military commands and for special occasions donned the vestments of the secular orders (Fig. 84). These were established as a way to decorate a man for outstanding state or civil service (Figs. 85, 86). Previously only military merit was honored with decorations.

The Order of St. Stephen (Fig. 87) was founded by Maria Theresa in 1764; the Order of Leopold (Figs. 88,

Fig. 81. Archdukes Joseph (center), Carl Joseph (right, in Hungarian dress), and Peter Leopold. Oil on canvas, about 1751–52. Schönbrunn Palace, Vienna. Inv. no. 2124.

Fig. 82. Emperor Joseph II (right) and his brother Grand Duke Peter Leopold of Tuscany in Rome in 1769. Oil on canvas, by Pompeo Batoni. Kunsthistorisches Museum, Vienna. Inv. no. 1628.

THE IMPERIAL STYLE

Fig. 83. Emperor Franz I in
the vestment of the Order
of the Golden Fleece. Oil
on canvas, about 1830, by
Friedrich von Amerling.
Schönbrunn Palace,
Vienna. Inv. no. 7545.

*Fig. 84. The vestments of knights of the orders of the Iron Crown, Leopold, and St. Stephen of Hungary. Kunsthistorisches Museum, Vienna. Photo: Joshua Greene.*

*Fig. 85. Vestment of a knight of the Order of the Golden Fleece. Mantle of dark red velvet embroidered in gold. The mantle bears a row of golden fleeces and the motto* Je l'ai empris *("I have accepted him"). The order was founded in 1429 in Bruges by Philip the Good, Duke of Burgundy, on the day of his wedding to Isabella of Portugal. It came under the control of the Hapsburgs through Mary, wife of Maximilian of Hapsburg and daughter of Charles the Bold, last of the dukes of Burgundy. The Order of the Golden Fleece rivaled the prestige of the Order of the Garter; only the very most aristocratic men received membership. The symbol of the order, the lamb, derives from the Greek myth of Jason and the biblical story of Gideon. The motto is* Ante ferit quam flamma micet *("First strike, then the flame will spring out"). Kunsthistorisches Museum, Vienna. Photo: Joshua Greene.*

89) was founded in 1806 by Franz I, who also renewed the Order of the Iron Crown (Fig. 91) in 1816. The details of the ostentatious vestments were prescribed by strict regulations; those of the Order of the Iron Crown were dictated down to the minutest detail.

Eventually it became necessary to create a court uniform for the lower offices and for diplomats as well as for those civilians who played a role in society and in politics. Court officials were first required to wear uniforms in 1793; by 1815 elaborate regulations prescribed uniforms for everyone at court.

Those who did not have the right to wear military or other uniforms continued to wear the court dress of the eighteenth century, which had hardly been affected at all by the vagaries of fashion. Another way to appear at court was in a national costume. This was a uniquely Austrian solution to the problem of appropriate court dress. The regional dress of the many Austrian states was sanctioned, and the requirement that one wear a uniform was neatly circumvented. This tradition is still honored; for example, when he is dressed in the so-called *Steireranzug*, a costume of the province of Styria,

*Fig. 86. Emperor Franz I conferring the Order of the Golden Fleece on two boys on the four hundredth anniversary of the founding of the order, May 22, 1830. Detail of a lithograph by Franz Wolf after J. N. Höchle. Kunsthistorisches Museum, Vienna. Inv. no. GS Z 11/2.*

THE IMPERIAL STYLE

Fig. 87. Vestment of a
knight of the Order of St.
Stephen of Hungary. Green
velvet mantle with full train
and oversleeves embroi-
dered in gold and trimmed
with bands of simulated
ermine. Scapular of red
velvet with gold embroi-
dery. Green velvet collar
with gold embroidery,
appliqué silver cross, and
simulated ermine border.
Hat (Kolpak) of dark red
velvet with gold embroi-

dery and simulated ermine
brim with egret aigrette.
Membership in the Order
of St. Stephen was limited
to one hundred men. Its
motto is Publicum meri-
torum praemium ("The
best for the public").
Kunsthistorisches Museum,
Vienna. Photo: Joshua
Greene.

an Austrian is acceptably dressed for even the grandest
social event. The most magnificent national costumes
are those of Hungary, often decorated with precious
stones and trimmed with fur (Fig. 90). However, the
costumes of Poland and Transylvania are hardly less
spectacular.

National costumes became intermingled with the
various uniforms and liveries of the court charges,
whose ranks and stations had to be clearly differen-
tiated. In German a *Hofstaat* (literally "court-state")
means the household of a prince. Actually the court was
an entire, self-contained sphere of life, with its own
jurisdiction and laws, governed by the court marshal,
the lord high chamberlain. In Vienna not only the
emperor had his own household; the empress had hers,
as did the crown prince. In the second half of the nineteenth century several of the lesser branches of the
house of Hapsburg had their own households and their
own court uniforms, which were often very elaborate.
Their staffs included their own aides-de-camp and
ladies-in-waiting, court officials, all types of liveried
servants, and coachmen. The imperial court was, of
course, much larger than any of the others, but it never
included more than a thousand persons. Even when
they were Holy Roman Emperors, the Hapsburg
emperors never had as many servants and officials as
did the kings of France.

The most important persons in the imperial household, those who had official duties at court, were the
lord high steward, the lord high treasurer, the lord high
chamberlain, and the master of the horse (Fig. 92). The
privy councillors, the chamberlains, and the high stew-
ards were also of this rank. Their titles were purely hon-
orary, however; they fulfilled no official function, yet
had to be present at court festivities. These events were
designated either "solemn" or "normal," which meant
that a man wore one of two different uniforms—either a
gala uniform or a uniform *à la campagne*. Within the
category of gala uniform a distinction was made
between "little gala" dress and the state uniform (Fig.
93). Finally there were regulations that pertained to
mourning clothes, which were divided into three
degrees of severity.

THE IMPERIAL STYLE

Fig. 88. Vestment of a knight of the Order of Leopold. White silk cape with gold embroidery and simulated ermine border. Collar of simulated ermine with appliqué star of the order. Pleated white cotton gauze ruff. Soft red velvet tunic with red metallic and tinsel embroidery. Breeches of soft red velvet with gold embroidery and tassels. Hat (Barett) of red velvet with gilt cords, ostrich plumes, and white ostrich aigrette. The motto of the order is Integritati et merito ("Integrity and merit"). Kunsthistorisches Museum, Vienna. Photo: Joshua Greene.

The next group of people at court were those appointed to official posts. Of the highest rank among these were the so-called *Edelknaben*, the pages. They were boys and young men of noble birth, but were essentially on the same level at court as the valets, porters, and lackeys (Fig. 94). All pages wore red uniforms, with gold trim signifying the lower ranks and gold embroidery the higher ranks.

The third group of court charges had important duties to fulfill, but did not have any official function at court and did not have to appear there. These were the civil servants in the offices of the court, the administrators of the various castles, the curators of the imperial collections, the concert master of the imperial orchestra, and the directors of the imperial theaters. They had gala uniforms only, since their sole function at court was to appear as background foils at large festivities. A special role was played by the equerries, who were in charge of the splendid gala carriages and the magnificent horses, as well as by the liveried coachmen and lackeys, who added much to the festive picture and glamour in the eyes of the public (Figs. 95, 96). Coachmen and lackeys were not dressed in red, but in black and yellow gala uniforms or in buff-colored uniforms *à la campagne*. They also appeared in so-called English livery on the occasions of the emperor's private drives in the city or sojourns in the country. These uniforms consisted of dark brown or black waistcoats, breeches, and top hats. The body guard, or *Leibjäger*, of the emperor or an archduke was the corps of lackeys who accompanied the official carriage. These men were splendidly dressed in silver and green and carried hunting horns and hunting swords in heavy leather bandaliers slung across their chests. The commanders of the lackeys and coachmen wore red tunics for gala occasions.

The collection of liveries in the Monturdepot presents an outstanding survey of court protocol of the second half of the nineteenth century. The last dress code of the Viennese court was that of 1894, and the uniforms in the collection reflect the taste of that time, which, as we have seen, had changed very little since the late eighteenth century.

*Fig. 89. The festive founding of the Order of Leopold at the Hofburg in 1808. In the left foreground are the knights of the Order of the Golden Fleece. In the center the newly decorated knights of the Order of Leopold stand while Emperor Franz I confers the order on an archduke. Detail of a lithograph by Franz Wolf after J. N. Höchle. Kunsthistorisches Museum, Vienna. Inv. no. GS Z 15/4.*

Fig. 90. National gala costume of a Hungarian aristocrat and the uniform of a royal Hungarian life guard. GALA COSTUME (left): Dark blue velvet mente *trimmed with mink. Turquoise and gold buttons. Dolman of cream-colored silk brocade trimmed with gold braid and frogging. Dark blue velvet cap trimmed with mink and gold soutache.* UNIFORM: *Red wool broadcloth tunic with silver soutache, galloon, and frogging. Leopard skin with silver buckles. Sash of green and silver-banded cords. Kunsthistorisches Museum, Vienna. Photo: Joshua Greene.*

Fig. 91. Vestment of a knight of the Order of the Iron Crown. Cape and collar of deep purple velvet with embroidery of silver thread and foil and an appliqué star of the order. White embroidered net ruff. Yellow orange tunic with silver embroidery. Purple velvet hat (Barett) with silver embroidery and white ostrich plume. The Order of the Iron Crown was founded by Napoleon after his coronation as king of the Lombards in 1805. The original badge of the order was a curved iron crown inscribed with the motto Dieu me l'a donnée, gare a qui y touchera ("God gave it to me. Beware he who would damage it"). After the fall of Napoleon, when Lombardy became part of the Austrian dominions, Emperor Franz I replaced the original badge with one whose motto, Avita et aucta ("Inherited and perpetuated"), is embroidered on these vestments. Kunsthistorisches Museum, Vienna. Photo: Joshua Greene.*

*Fig. 92. Master of the Horse Fürst Johann zu Trautsmannsdorff leaving the Hofburg. He wears a gala uniform; his horse is covered with the so-called* Kröningswaldrappe *(coronation saddle blanket). Oil on canvas, 1814, by Sigismund von Perger. Kunsthistorisches Museum, Vienna. Photo: Meyer, Vienna.*

THE IMPERIAL STYLE

*Fig. 93. Gala banquet at court, Schönbrunn Palace, to celebrate the centennial, in 1858, of the founding of the military order of Maria Theresa. The officers of the Viennese garrison rise for the toast proposed by Emperor Franz Joseph I. Wall painting, by Siegmund l'Allemand. Schönbrunn Palace, Vienna. Photo: Meyer, Vienna.*

THE IMPERIAL STYLE

*Fig. 94. Detail of Fig. 93. Footmen attending the diners.*

*Fig. 95. Gala winter livery of a groom or footman. Greatcoat (Kaputrock) of black wool trimmed with golden yellow galloon. Kunsthistorisches Museum, Vienna. Photo: Joshua Greene.*

*Fig. 96. An imperial light carriage and four à la Daumont in the park of Schönbrunn Palace. Mounted are one forerider, two jockeys, and two lackeys. Oil on canvas, about 1860. Kunsthistorisches Museum, Vienna.*

*Fig. 97. Three spencers from postilions' gala livery. Kunsthistorisches Museum, Vienna. Photos: Udo F. Sitzenfrey, Vienna.*

THE IMPERIAL STYLE

*Fig. 98. Coat of a rider of the Spanish Riding School. Dark brown wool twill. Spanische Hofreitschule, Vienna. Photo: Joshua Greene.*

*Fig. 99. Greatcoat of a captain of the life guard, dismounted. White wool broadcloth with red collar and piping. Kunsthistorisches Museum, Vienna. Photo: Joshua Greene.*

# Empress Elisabeth, 1837–1898

By Brigitte Hamann

Sisi's life was a legend. Empress Elisabeth of Austria, queen of Hungary and Bohemia, was the fairy-tale beauty portrayed by Winterhalter with diamond stars in her long, chestnut brown hair (Fig. 100). She was a creature of luxury, adorned with the crown jewels and with the most expensive clothes, embroidered with precious stones and pearls.

The film industry of the twentieth century has played a major part in creating this beautiful legend. The truth is much less romantic. Her beauty was hardly a blessing for the empress; it was the source of many neuroses and fears, and maintaining it took many hours each day—hours that could have been put to better use. Her struggle to retain her beauty kept Elisabeth away from many important duties. Aging made her shy, turned her into a recluse who anxiously hid her face behind umbrellas and fans.

Elisabeth, born Christmas Eve, 1837, in Munich, descended from a minor branch of the Bavarian royal family of Wittelsbach. She was not a princess, but only a "duchess in Bavaria." Her upbringing among seven brothers and sisters was by no means courtly. "Duke Max in Bavaria" let his children grow up naturally and with much freedom. They spent the winters in Munich and the summers at the idyllic Possenhofen castle on the Tegernsee. The children had many pets. They rode well. They took long hikes through the Bavarian mountains. They knew how to fish, dance, fence, and make a little music. They knew little of fashion or elegance, but were dressed more like farmers' children, who tore their stockings and clothes while playing their wild games. A series of teachers was hired for them, but Duke Max did not think highly of erudition, and neither did his children. Throughout her life Elisabeth looked back on her youth—the freedom and closeness to nature she enjoyed in her childhood—as a paradise lost.

The story of her engagement is well known. Elisabeth's mother and the mother of Emperor Franz Joseph I were sisters. Since it was mandatory that the emperor marry a Catholic princess and Archduchess Sophie, Franz Joseph's mother, preferred a niece to a stranger as a daughter-in-law, the sisters agreed that the twenty-three-year-old emperor would marry eighteen-year-old Helene, Elisabeth's older sister. The young couple was to get to know each other better at the imperial summer retreat at Ischl in the summer of 1853 and then become engaged.

Duchess Ludovika took her second daughter, fifteen-year-old "Sisi," along on that memorable trip to Ischl. Despite avid searching, no suitable match had been found for Elisabeth. The duchess had inquired at the court of Saxony, but had had to stipulate that her younger daughter would not have a large dowry and was rather "fresh, but had not a single pretty feature." She now hoped to win Franz Joseph's younger brother for Sisi. The girl came to Ischl unaffected and still rather childlike, and her wardrobe for the trip was of course much less elaborate than her sister's.

The young emperor's first encounter with his Bavarian cousins did not go according to plan. As usual, Duchess Ludovika arrived late. She had had migraine headaches en route and had had to interrupt her journey. Besides that, when she and her daughters finally did arrive, it was without their maids and luggage. All three ladies were in mourning, since an aunt had died recently, and the coach with their gala dresses had been delayed so that they could not change clothes before the decisive encounter. Archduchess Sophie sent her personal maid to the hotel to coif the ladies; great care was taken that Helene's hair was done perfectly, but no one looked after little Sisi, who put up her own long hair.

Franz Joseph met his cousins at afternoon tea. From the first moment he was interested only in little Elisabeth, who sat at the table, unsuspecting and unabashed, watching Helene and the emperor with curiosity. The confusion of the two mothers grew from encounter to encounter. Finally Helene's gala dresses arrived, and the girl shone in a silk ball gown embroidered in gold. Sisi wore a simple pink muslin gown, but, just as in a fairy tale, all the emperor's attention was on the younger sister.

Elisabeth reacted to the unexpected courtship of the emperor with shyness and embarrassment. Archduchess Sophie reprimanded her sister for arriving late and for dressing Helene in black, which made the tall, dark girl look even more severe. Ludovika countered, "The emperor seems to really love Sisi. If only she can give him what he needs!" Helene sat stoically by as the plan for her future dissolved.

The engagement was announced from Ischl. The little girl from the country was to be the bride of the most desirable bachelor of the nineteenth century. Gradually she realized what was happening to her and finally said faintheartedly: "I do love him very much. If only he were not an emperor!" Sisi's trousseau was assembled in a great hurry and her bridal wardrobe sewn in even greater haste. The Bavarian tailors, shoemakers, and embroiderers enjoyed a business boom. The little girl received her first fine clothes; Franz Joseph visited his fiancée several times in Bavaria and brought her magnificent pins, rings, and necklaces and a blue velvet coat and muff lined with sable. A month before the wedding he presented her with a luxurious diamond diadem, a gift from Archduchess Sophie, who had worn it on her own wedding day.

However, the young bride showed little interest in all the beautiful things. The tailors complained that she hardly took time to try on their handiwork; she was happiest when she was out of doors in her old clothes, and she considered all the new luxuries strange. Sisi was still a child; her favorite gift from the emperor was a parrot he sent to Bavaria.

Sisi's family anxiously observed that she seemed flattered by her success, but that she grew quieter and more melancholy at the same time. She often locked herself in her room and wrote sad poems about the imminent loss of her freedom. Obviously she was afraid of entering the sophisticated world of the Viennese court. She was also afraid of her aunt and mother-in-law, Sophie, who constantly criticized her. Sophie even sent Elisabeth a letter admonishing her to take better care of her teeth. For the rest of her life Elisabeth avoided opening her mouth too far when she talked or laughed. She mumbled so badly that she could hardly be understood.

Elisabeth's education, which had been neglected for fifteen years, had to be accomplished in the few months before the wedding. Foreign languages had to be learned, as well as the history of the house of Hapsburg and the protocol of the Viennese court. Dance instructors, coiffeurs, tailors, and, above all, painters attended the young girl. Everyone wanted to know what the future empress of Austria looked like. Two portraits of Elisabeth on horseback were made as Christmas presents for the emperor.

The inventory of Sisi's trousseau has survived in the Court and State Archive in Vienna. At the time of her marriage she owned jewelry in the value of 100,000 florins. However, if one looks closely at the list, one realizes that about ninety percent of the pieces were gifts from Franz Joseph or his mother. The most valuable article was Sophie's wedding diadem of diamonds and opals with a matching necklace and earrings, valued at 60,000 florins. A bracelet of diamonds set with a miniature portrait of the emperor, estimated at 10,000 florins, was a gift from Franz Joseph, as were five diamond pins, two hairpins set with diamonds and emeralds, and a matching bracelet and earrings of diamonds and sapphires. Very modest in comparison was a bracelet of blue enamel with the slogan "God with you" set in diamonds. This gift from Elisabeth's mother was valued at 170 florins.

Her wedding silver was more than modest; it was practically nonexistent. The total value of the meticulously enumerated washbasins, plates, and mirrors came to no more than 700 florins. And this was at a time when silver formed the heart of an upper-class girl's dowry.

Sisi's wardrobe, on the other hand, was quite valuable — evaluated at nearly 50,000 florins. Sisi brought the following articles of clothing to Vienna with her: seventeen *Putzkleider* (evening dresses with trains); her wedding dress with a manteau of silver moiré; a gold embroidered tulle dress with an embroidered white moiré manteau; three dresses in blue, pink, and green Brussels lace with trains; a blue silk dress with black lace; dresses of green and white damask embroidered in pink and white; a pink and a white dress, each with a train; and a festive black dress of *moiré antique* for court mourning. There were also

Fig. 101. Emperor Franz
Joseph I and Empress
Elisabeth at the time of
their marriage. Painting on
porcelain, 1854. Hofburg,
Vienna.

three other silk dresses with two bodices each and eleven *montant* dresses in green, sky blue, violet, pink, brown, and black.

The bride had six morning coats: one of colorful cashmere, two of silk, one of plush, two of white material, one with English embroidery, the other decorated with guipure. The nineteen summer dresses, decorated with *pensées*, were ornamented with roses, violets, and stars made of straw and grains of corn, and were further decorated with flounces, ribbons, and guipure. There were only four ball gowns: two in white, one decorated with gold lace, the other with silver lace; one pink gown with blonde lace and fringes; and one light blue gown trimmed with roses.

As accessories to the dresses there were the so-called *Putz-Gegenstände* (hair ornaments), among them twelve "coiffures"; two white-feather hairdresses, one with red roses, the other with silver leaves; one pink-feather headdress with apple blossoms; others bore laces, ribbons, pearls, and artificial flowers. There were ten flower arrangements made up of all sorts of blossoms, from lilies of the valley to roses, forget-me-nots, and hyacinths, and eight other flower wreaths. There were sixteen hats: two white ones and one pink one made of feathers; one Florentine straw hat with blue plumes; four other straw hats; many lace bonnets; black, gray, and brown riding hats with feathers; and four gauze veils. Even a garden hat with a garland of field flowers is listed; Sisi had worn it to the Sunday mass at which the emperor announced the engagement.

Also in the trousseau were fifteen pieces of lace, mostly in white, black, and silver made into mantillas, jackets, shawls, and veils. Sisi had six coats: one embroidered in white and gold; two cashmere coats, one in blue, the other embroidered in gray; and three velvet coats (one brown; one dark blue with black feather trim; and the velvet one given to her by her fiancé). There were eight mantillas of velvet, silk, and moiré to wear with evening dresses and five other mantelets. Two of these were cashmere embroidered with pink and white. A pink mantelet with silver threads woven into it was the one Sisi wore for her arrival at

Fig. 103. Elisabeth and her
mother entering Vienna
before the imperial wed-
ding, April 23, 1854.
Lithograph, 1854, by F.
Kollârz. Museen der Stadt
Wien. Inv. no. 65.579.
Photo: Rudolf Stepanck,
Vienna.

Vienna. The inventory also lists a white one with gold thread woven into it. There were five *écharpes* in white, pink, blue, and black. There were also five "Turkish" shawls, ten square neckerchiefs, and five long shawls.

Even the lingerie is listed precisely: there were "chemisettes with sleeves," many of them of Valenciennes lace or guipure, and twelve riding chemisettes — a total of 144 chemises of lace-trimmed batiste and thirty-six nightgowns, twelve of them with long sleeves. Twenty-four riding shirts also appear on the list.

There were fourteen dozen stockings of silk and cotton, seventeen dozen handkerchiefs of four different qualities, ten bed jackets of muslin and silk, twelve embroidered nightcaps, three negligée-caps of embroidered muslin, twelve hairnets of colored silk, twenty-four neckerchiefs for the nightgowns, and twelve little linen scarfs. Sisi brought six dozen petticoats to Vienna with her. These were of piqué, flannel, and silk. There were also three crinolines, five dozen linen and flannel "trousers," twenty-four combing jackets, four corsets — one, of white moiré, was for the wedding dress — three riding corsets, fourteen corset covers of batiste and tulle with lace, three bathing shirts, and three flannel bathrobes.

The number of shoes was sizable: eighteen pairs of black "Trunell" boots, six pairs of black velvet boots, six pairs of black riding boots, six pairs of brown cloth boots and another six pairs in gray, six pairs of boots of bronze-colored leather, and fifteen pairs of silk and satin boots, twenty-four pairs of white and twenty-four pairs of black satin shoes, eight pairs of slippers, among which were one pink and one silver pair, and, finally, three pairs of rubber boots. It seems however, that Elisabeth hadn't enough shoes. She had hardly arrived in Vienna before a good number of pairs had to be made for her — at the unusually high cost of 700 florins. (It is true that traditionally the empress of Austria wore her shoes only once and they were then given away. It was a custom Sisi never liked and later abolished.) The bride brought with her twenty dozen pairs of gloves — 240 pairs — among which six dozen were white.

L'IRIS

Journal de Modes et d'Arts

VIe Année.    N° 16. 1854.

Portrait de S. M. Elisabeth Duchesse de Bavière, Impératrice d'Autriche.

Among the "other objects" noted in the inventory are two fans (remarkably few), two umbrellas, and three large and two small parasols. Even tortoiseshell combs, dress-, hair-, nail-, and toothbrushes as well as shoe-horns are listed, as is a box containing pins and hair-pins, ribbons, and buttons. All this was brought to Vienna before the wedding in fourteen large trunks. It was a sizable trousseau for a "duchess in Bavaria," but it was very modest by the standards of the ostentatious Viennese court. As empress of Austria, Sisi was to spend 20,000 to 30,000 florins a year for her toilette alone. One of her first acquisitions after the wedding was a Hungarian court train for 400 florins and a bright red cashmere shawl for 450 florins.

Some of the Viennese society ladies had turned up their noses upon hearing of the engagement; the emperor was bringing an unknown little duchess home to Vienna — it was not a brilliant match at all. Everyone had heard that the empress was very young, but nothing had been said about her beauty or elegance. Stories circulated about how Duke Max had let his children grow up wild. It was said that they rode like circus performers, but that they could not put together a French sentence, let alone "converse" at court — and the parquet of the Viennese court was reputedly slippery.

Four days before the wedding, on April 20, 1854, the now sixteen-year-old Sisi tearfully left her native city of Munich. Six horses drew her coach. Sisi sat in the back seat in a dark riding habit, and next to her was her very excited mother. In the front her sisters sat crowded together: the dejected Helene, the young Marie (later queen of Naples), Sophie (at one time the fiancée of King Ludwig II of Bavaria), and Mathilde. Her brother Karl Theodor sat on the trestle next to the coachman. In a second coach, drawn by only two horses, her father followed with her two other brothers.

The family accompanied Sisi to Straubing on the Danube, where the bride-to-be and her mother boarded the boat *Franz Joseph*, which brought them down the river to Vienna. The journey was a triumph for the future empress of Austria. All the towns and villages along the river were festively decorated. Bands played and cheering crowds lined the riverbanks. In Linz, the first stop on Austrian soil, Elisabeth was met by Franz Joseph, who had traveled west to unofficially welcome her. In Linz Sisi set foot on Austrian soil for the first time and was honored by cannon salutes and the tolling of church bells. She was greeted by little girls dressed in white and received by all the city dignitaries. After spending the night, Sisi continued her journey to Vienna. The emperor, conscientious as always, had left at half past four in the morning on the fastest steamboat so that he could receive Sisi for a second time, in Vienna. Her arrival there was marked by all the pomp and circumstance of the imperial city, and with the diplomatic corps, the officials of the church, the aristocracy, the court ministers, and civil servants in attendance.

Archduchess Sophie stepped aboard the boat right behind her son to greet the prospective bride. From that moment on, little Sisi was a personage of state, observed by a thousand critical eyes. At first the dignitaries were thrilled: the bride was a girl, still very self-conscious, very pale and shy, but of fairylike beauty and charm. Sisi disembarked in bright sunshine wearing her pink silk gown with a white mantelet and a little white bonnet. Her full, light brown hair was done up simply. She was quite as tall as the emperor and extremely slender.

The joy the Viennese took in their new empress was sincere. Franz Joseph had been ruling for six years by the time of his marriage. The first lady of the empire had been his mother, an energetic, strict, and devout woman, who did not enhance the brilliance of the Viennese court. Before Franz Joseph acceded in the year of the revolution, 1848, the tone at court had been even more dismal. Emperor Ferdinand ("the Benevolent"), an epileptic, and his unhappy wife had been quite overshadowed by Chancellor Klemens von Metternich. Thus the Viennese had been waiting a long time for a proper empress — one who could give the Austrian court the elegance that the beautiful Empress Eugénie, wife of Napoleon III, had produced in Paris. The two imperial courts, Paris and Vienna, presided over by these beautiful empresses, were to become

*Fig. 105. The imperial family in Hungarian costume. The children pictured are Gisela and Rudolf. Lithograph, about 1860.Austrian National Library, Vienna. Inv. no. NB 510.520.*

*Fig. 106. An official portrait of the empress at twenty-seven. Oil on canvas, 1863, by Franz Russ. Kunsthistorisches Museum, Vienna. Inv. no. 7134.*

rival centers of European fashion. Vienna was finally to catch up with Paris, which had previously always been in the lead.

Elaborate ceremonies had been planned in connection with the wedding, and Sisi had to learn her part hurriedly. Chased from one reception to the next, in a new, pompous environment among unfamiliar and critical people, Elisabeth burst into tears again and again. She was even crying when she stepped into the glass coach, drawn by eight white horses, that brought her across the newly constructed Elisabeth Bridge to the inner city. The procession was headed by a division of uhlans (lancers), and several *fouriers* on horseback, all in magnificent uniforms, followed by sixty pairs of royal and imperial chamberlains and court councillors also on horseback. The Hungarian magnates followed in their costumes of velvet and silk ornamented with heavy gold embroidery and precious stones and accompanied by their liveried servants and their own hussars. Behind the court dignitaries on horseback came fifteen gala coaches, each drawn by six horses. These were accompanied by splendidly liveried servants, all wearing white wigs, led by two runners in *Baretts* with tall plumes. These in turn were followed by court trumpeters on horseback, pages *(Edelknaben)*, the trabant guard with their flags, and a host of high dignitaries in traditional uniforms that little Sisi could not tell apart. Cannons boomed, flags waved, the bells of all the churches in Vienna tolled, and a rejoicing crowd thronged the streets.

Sisi sat next to her mother (Fig. 103). She wore a pink satin dress, the fabric interwoven with silver thread, and a long train embroidered with garlands of roses. A lace *écharpe* lay around her shoulders. In her hair she wore a wreath of red and white roses and the magnificent new diamond diadem. The diadem caught on the door of her gala coach when she tried to step down, and this added to her nervousness. As many observers noticed, the child was simply overtaxed.

At the wedding, which took place in the Augustinerkirche on April 24, 1854, at seven o'clock in the evening, the bride was solemn and deathly pale. She was led to the altar where the emperor waited with her

mother and her prospective mother-in-law. Elisabeth wore a white dress of *moiré antique* heavily embroidered with gold and silver (Fig. 104), and with it a heavy white coat embroidered in gold, with a long train. The coat was held at the shoulders with large diamond brooches. The veil of Brussels lace was fastened to the diamond diadem by a bridal wreath of fresh myrtles and orange blossoms. On her left side Elisabeth wore her new orders: the royal Bavarian Order of Theresa, the Russian imperial, and the Austrian imperial Star-Cross Order. Around her neck she wore a collar of diamonds and opals that matched the diadem;

THE IMPERIAL STYLE

Fig. 107. An intimate
portrait of Elisabeth.
Oil on canvas, 1861, by
Franz Xaver Winterhalter.
Kunsthistorisches Museum,
Vienna. Inv. no. 9142.

several diamond bouquets secured the bows and trimmings on her dress. On her bosom, among all the
jewels, the flower-loving Elisabeth wore a bouquet of
fresh roses.

After the ceremony a great reception was held in the
Hofburg. The diplomatic corps and all the court dignitaries filed past the young empress, kissed her hand,
and congratulated her. Elisabeth was embarrassed
and uneasy. In the evening, the young couple drove
through Vienna in the imperial equipage with its gold-
plated wheels and received the adoration of the people
of Vienna. The streets of the capital and the great palaces of the aristocracy were festively lit and decorated.

At last the great day was over. Sisi was exhausted
when her mother took her to bed. Twelve pages with
golden candelabra led the way; the chatelaine and four
maids accompanied them. Half an hour later there was
a knock at the door; Archduchess Sophie brought the
groom to the sixteen-year-old bride. The next day everyone knew that Franz Joseph had "spared" the girl on
the first night. Everyone also knew — through whatever
obscure channels — that Sisi had finally become his wife
on the third night. There were no intimacies at court.
The morning after the consummation the young couple
breakfasted with Archduchess Sophie. Elisabeth had
resisted attending the breakfast, but the young
emperor was too used to listening to his mother — he
himself had known court protocol since childhood — to
allow his young wife to have her only too understandable wish. Elisabeth never forgave her husband or her
mother-in-law this breakfast. She returned to her
apartments in tears, deserted by her husband, who had
business to attend to, and left to the mercy of strangers.
Her own family had returned to Bavaria after the wedding; not a single confidante had been allowed to
remain with the empress. Elisabeth had her own court
staff, with a chatelaine and a chamberlain, two ladies-
in-waiting, a secretary, a lady's maid, two grooms, one
*portier*, four personal lackeys, one porter, and one
housemaid. All these people were middle aged and
were hand-picked by Archduchess Sophie. Sisi could
not confide in any of them, because she assumed — cor-
rectly — that all of them were her mother-in-law's spies.

There was no hope of a wedding trip for the young
imperial couple. Delegations from every part of the
empire arrived to pay their respects to the new
empress. For every reception Elisabeth had to learn a
new protocol.

Sisi, who had been used to the freedom of her Bavarian home and a noisy and tolerant family, felt locked in a
gilded cage. She became almost ill with homesickness
and soon began writing melancholy poems. Only days
after her wedding she regretted her "vain" move to
Vienna. That was the bitter beginning of a marriage for
which there were hardly better days ahead.

Reluctantly — after many lectures from her mother-
in-law and as many fights for her freedom — Sisi began
to follow the rules of the Viennese court. The jewels and
the beautiful clothes were a burden to her, since
choosing them and trying them on was another ceremony. There were fights about the smallest things: Sisi
refused to give away her shoes after a single wearing.
She did not like being dressed by her servants and
particularly hated being helped with her lingerie and
stockings. She was very shy, and the maids were
strangers. Besides, she had been raised to be independent. The chambermaids turned up their noses; the
empress did not know the simplest rules — those that
had been *en vogue* at the court for centuries.

Only her animals were a comfort to Sisi. She especially loved her parrots and spent many hours with
them. When, two months after the wedding, there
were signs of pregnancy, Archduchess Sophie recommended that even the parrots be taken away from the
young empress, lest she bear a child that resembled a
parrot from having looked at one too much. Sisi now
abided this and similar prohibitions by her mother-in-
law without a fight, but she was full of silent rage. Her
deep resentment of Sophie developed at this time, as
did her lifelong persecution complex. Elisabeth complained until the end of her life of the loneliness and
desperation of her first weeks of marriage.

Sisi's lack of success in society and at the endless *cer-
cles* is not surprising, since she spoke no foreign languages. Under the circumstances an obviously "nonaristocratic" upbringing was fatal, even for an empress.

Her ignorance of protocol made the young empress
practically an outcast at court, where she had few followers at the beginning. Almost no one had any sym-
pathy for this unhappy girl, ill with homesickness, who
was forced to play the role of empress of one of the
largest empires in the world. Elisabeth never forgot the
isolation she felt. The Viennese nobility was odious to
her all her life. Later she did everything in her power
to provoke them, and her son, Rudolf, followed her
example.

The first child was a girl. Its godmother was, of
course, Archduchess Sophie, for whom the child was
named without Elisabeth ever having been consulted.
Elisabeth was now seventeen and was supposedly not
mature enough to bring up her child; that function was
taken over by the old archduchess. The young empress
rebelled in vain when the baby was quartered, with its
own attendants, in the apartments of its grandmother,
far from Elisabeth's rooms. The heavy dresses with
voluminous crinolines made the walks through the
drafty rooms and up over narrow stairs difficult for
Elisabeth, who was pregnant again very soon. The
emperor, in a letter to his mother, remarked that poor
Sisi had to "wheeze" up the stairs in order to see her
child. The visits became more infrequent. The
upbringing of the next two children, Gisela and Rudolf
(little Sophie died in 1857), was the same (Fig. 105).
Elisabeth never had close contact with her older children. Only with her fourth — Valerie, born in 1868 —
was she able to get her way. This child grew up under
her mother's care.

The public knew nothing of these family tragedies.
They only saw Sisi's grace and beauty. She grew riper
and more beautiful with every child. She retained her
slender figure and gained self-assurance and elegance.

Elisabeth wore the fullest crinolines with great grace
and preferred the finest materials for her clothes. A dip-
lomat who sat next to her at dinner complained jokingly
that he had not sat next to her, but under her; that is
how full her dress had been. She particularly liked to
wear national costumes. In Hungary she made herself
very popular by wearing a richly embroidered cap,
tightly laced bodice, lace apron, and full, embroidered

skirt. For the hikes in the mountains that she loved — in Tirol, for instance — she wore a short loden skirt, simple blouse, loose jacket, knitted woolen socks, hiking boots, and little loden hat with a feather. The Tiroleans were delighted by this tribute to their regional dress. However, Elisabeth's own mood of despair never lifted.

The emperor too was despondent; he had great political difficulties and had a military defeat in Italy to contend with as well as his domestic problems. Foreign diplomats hinted at a crisis in the imperial marriage — even of infidelity on the part of the emperor. The twenty-two-year-old empress became seriously ill with a mysterious ailment, which was sometimes described as a disease of the lungs. Her condition became so serious after an acute attack in the winter of 1860 that Elisabeth left her family and went as far away as possible — to the island of Madeira. She refused to remain on the soil of the monarchy — in Merano or Venice.

Her departure was sudden. A yacht borrowed from Queen Victoria of England took the young empress from Antwerp to Madeira. The public was astonished; her abrupt leave-taking and remote destination caused general confusion. The official statements of the physicians were more than vague and immediately gave rise to fantastic rumors that are still repeated: the emperor had infected his young wife with venereal disease and she could no longer bear his company. It is possible, of course, that Elisabeth feigned the illness (or that she only imagined herself to be ill) in order to flee the depressing atmosphere of Vienna and her husband, who may have deceived her. There is no question that she was relieved to put distance between herself and her mother-in-law, who was the real empress of Austria and against whom Sisi had no power.

The empress left Austria in November. Her youngest child, Crown Prince Rudolf, was two years old. Her fairy-tale marriage was in tatters, but only the inner circle at court knew the truth; the population believed that the empress was actually ill.

Sisi stayed in Madeira for six months. The emperor had granted her unlimited credit, and she had with her a large staff of servants, a few familiar ladies-in-waiting (whom she had picked herself), and a very handsome officer, who promptly fell in love with her and whom she rebuffed. On Madeira she was cut off from the world. Mail boats arrived infrequently, but the emperor regularly sent couriers, who were to report to him on his wife's condition. According to the couriers' reports, the empress's health was precarious. She wept often and spent her days playing cards, walking on the lush green island, reading, and engaged in mindless games with her ladies. She kept six ponies. Otherwise there were few diversions.

Once a Russian naval ship docked, and the young empress invited all the officers to shore for dinner and a dance. A Russian admiral later reported that every officer — young and old — had fallen in love with the young empress. Elisabeth's self-confidence had grown. She received the Russians' attention as a tribute due her and never compromised herself in any way. In every situation she remained the empress — the lofty, beautiful, untouchable woman who did not descend to the level of others.

After half a year's absence from Vienna, Elisabeth viewed her husband differently. She used her beauty confidently and very energetically against him. And he retreated. Elisabeth returned to Vienna for four weeks in 1861, but the symptoms of her "illness" promptly returned. Receptions, dinners, and other functions were cancelled, and Elisabeth demanded to leave again. The story circulated at court that she locked her door to the emperor and complained of migraine headaches. Finally she fled again — without any argument from her husband. This time she went to the Greek island of Corfu. Later she returned to her Bavarian home, then visited various spas in Germany.

It was a great strain for Elisabeth to remain at court in Vienna between trips. She avoided not only her mother-in-law, but also the Austrian aristocracy whenever she could. She did not join her husband at most official functions, yet he protested only mildly, perhaps because of a guilty conscience, perhaps because of the favors she occasionally did grant him. Sisi considered herself a misunderstood woman, and, as she grew more and more egocentric, she fled more often from the calamity of her marriage. In time she became the symbol of misunderstood, frustrated wives everywhere, who, however, did not have the good fortune to be empresses with unlimited credit and endlessly generous husbands.

Elisabeth allowed her older children, Gisela and Rudolf, to grow up under the supervision of their grandmother. By her constant absences she was not only a bad wife and mother, but also an ineffective empress. She spent her time busily constructing her own legend, which remains in effect today.

She made the maintenance of her beauty into a rite. The care of her chestnut-brown hair, which reached to her knees, took several hours each day; washing it took an entire day. New products to keep it healthy and make it shiny were constantly being tried. Elisabeth's hairdresser, Feifalik, became indispensable to the empress on her journeys. In order to have her nearby at all times Sisi married the hairdresser off to another member of her staff. Frau Feifalik knew how to deal with Elisabeth, who was upset about every hair that was lost during her morning combing: she attached a strip of adhesive tape to the underside of her apron and hastily tucked away the fallen hair.

Elisabeth also spent hours every day at her toilette. She shocked the court by having a bathroom installed in the Hofburg. Previously there had never been a bathroom in either the imperial residence or in the 1,200-room Schönbrunn Palace. As time went by, Elisabeth acquired some rather unusual grooming habits. Every morning she took a cold shower followed by a massage, and on some evenings, claiming a headache, she excused herself from official dinners and took long oil baths to smoothe her skin. Sisi was the only woman at court who had her own bath maid, a woman who even accompanied her on her journeys. The cosmetic industry had not yet been developed, and one relied on handmade natural products. Sisi was always informed of the newest developments in this field. She had strange mixtures concocted according to old Indian recipes: for a time she used enormous amounts of strawberry cream on her face. At another time she washed only with lemon juice and required twenty slightly moldy lemons daily — which greatly embar-

rassed her staff, especially when she was traveling in foreign countries. She did gymnastic exercises daily and exercised with dumbells, worked on the rings, and used the balance beam and other apparatus. Her exercise room in the Hofburg and the one she had installed in her hunting castle, the "Hermesvilla," are still popular tourist attractions.

Elisabeth checked her weight every day on a decimal scale in her exercise room and fasted as soon as she had gained a fraction of a pound. In the course of time she became anoretic. She could only tolerate thin people in her presence and ate almost nothing except the juice squeezed from meat and now and then a little violet sherbet or oranges. After her death, the doctors who examined the body found that she suffered from severe starvation edema.

Stories about the beauty of the Austrian empress went around Europe and the world from the 1860s on. Winterhalter painted two famous portraits of her in 1864–65. One of these shows the empress in a white ball gown with diamond stars in her braided hair (Fig. 100); the other, a very intimate portrait, which Emperor Franz Joseph kept over his desk until his death, shows her with her hair down, in a simple white negligée without any jewelry. When Winterhalter showed sketches for these paintings to Empress Eugénie in Paris, she reacted by calling Elisabeth, who was twelve years her junior, the most beautiful crowned head in Europe, an honor that had been Eugénie's until then.

Over the years Sisi learned how to use her beauty to gain her goals, particularly when she wanted something from her husband, who was more in love than ever with his beautiful wife. In 1865, for instance, Sisi managed to effect a change in the kind of education her son, Rudolf, received. The military drilling, which had exhausted the little boy and made him seriously ill, was stopped after Sisi's intervention. She recommended and got for her son a middle-class liberal education, and Rudolf was grateful to his mother for the rest of his life.

As an outward sign of his adoration the emperor spoiled his wife with jewelry of all sorts. The most precious piece in Sisi's legendary collection was a three-

strand necklace of natural pearls, which she received on Rudolf's birthday. In 1858 it was valued at 75,000 florins. The empress's jewelry collection grew over the years until it was one of the most opulent in Europe, even the world, with an estimated value of five million florins. Since Elisabeth's favorite jewel was the emerald, she owned fabulous rings, brooches, necklaces, and diadems containing this stone. (The emperor was also very generous to his mistress, the actress Katharina Schratt. She too acquired a famous jewelry collection, which was sold at auction after her death.)

At last Archduchess Sophie's influence began to wane in proportion to the slow but steady increase in Elisabeth's power. In 1867 Sisi enjoyed her greatest triumph. After Austria lost the war to Prussia, at a point when the monarchy of the Danube states threatened to collapse, the empress used her beauty politically for the first and only time: she supported the political equality of the Hungarians within the monarchy, and managed to have her husband crowned king of Hungary.

The Hungarians who had wanted to secede from the monarchy after the revolution of 1848, and who had similar desires after the defeat of 1866, now found a champion in the Austrian empress. She allowed herself to be captivated by the chivalry and elegance of the Magyar aristocracy, by the generosity of their life-style, and by their desire for freedom. Years earlier Elisabeth had studied Hungarian avidly, just to vex Archduchess Sophie, who hated the Hungarians.

As Sisi's position at court grew stronger, so did the Hungarian influence in Vienna. To the chagrin of the Viennese aristocracy Elisabeth gathered more and more Hungarians around her. Eventually she had only Hungarian ladies-in-waiting; finally even a Hungarian chamberlain was employed. In 1864 a young, nonaristocratic girl named Ida Ferenczy had joined Elisabeth's staff as the official "reader," but the girl was actually a close friend and confidante. Sisi liked Ida because she could trust her and because the girl was in close communication with the Hungarian politician Gyula Andrássy.

Andrássy, fourteen years older than Elisabeth, had had an adventurous life: he had been a revolutionary in 1848, had fled to Paris, in Austria had been condemned to death by hanging during his absence (he had become known as "le beau pendu" in Paris society). He returned triumphant to Budapest in the 1860s and became the leader of the moderate liberals who supported a coalition with Austria and were against the Hungarian independence promoted by Lajos Kossuth. From 1867 until 1871 Andrássy was the president of the Hungarian cabinet; from 1871 to 1879 he served as foreign minister of Austria-Hungary. He was a wiry and slender man of somewhat Gypsy-like good looks, full of temperament, impulsive, witty — everything but pedantic. He was a famous lady-killer, but was also the devoted father of four children. He was the great love of Elisabeth's life, but it was an unfulfilled love — perhaps the more romantic for that. Sisi, disappointed in her marriage and very unexperienced as a woman, came entirely under Andrássy's spell in the mid-1860s. Ida Ferenczy delivered letters and messages between the two. They saw each other seldom and then always in their official capacities. The letters they wrote were not · billet-doux, but dealt with political matters. Andrássy, who adored the beautiful empress, but who was a politician first, saw a chance to gain his political ends through the young empress, and in this he was totally successful. Sisi had never been interested in politics before. Only now, where the fate of Hungary (and Andrássy's will) was involved did she become politically active. She was instrumental in effecting the total change in Austria in 1867, through which it became a "royal and imperial" state. The Austrian Empire was transformed into a unique system of government, the double monarchy of Austria-Hungary, in which Germans and Magyars shared the power. The other nations of the monarchy, especially the Slavs, were very much repressed. The people of Bohemia demanded that Franz Joseph be crowned king of Bohemia, but they struggled in vain; Elisabeth did not intervene on their behalf. Her power at this point can be gathered from the fact that the emperor acted against his own better judgment — and against the advice of his mother — giving in with great reluctance to everything that his beautiful wife and Andrássy demanded.

The coronation of Franz Joseph as king of Hungary in June 1867 was the climax of Elisabeth's life. She was twenty-nine years old and more beautiful than ever before or after. With Andrássy's help she became queen of Hungary. Her Austrian ladies-in-waiting remarked maliciously that "she was as serious... during the coronation as a bride at her wedding." In fact the splendor of the coronation festivities in Budapest surpassed by far the wedding of the imperial couple. Sisi's dress was the most precious creation she had ever worn. It came from the French couture house of Worth (ordinarily Elisabeth bought her dresses from the Viennese salon Spitzer) and was modeled on the Hungarian national gala costume (Fig. 108). It consisted of a white dress richly embroidered in silver with a black velvet bodice laced with heavy strings of pearls. Under this was a white blouse with puffed sleeves. A magnificent white lace apron and a full skirt with a long train completed the ensemble. Elisabeth wore her richest jewelry on this occasion. A white lace veil was fastened to the back of her head with a diamond crown. Even the emperor was so taken with the "transcendental" beauty of his wife that he embraced her spontaneously in front of all the ladies-in-waiting when he saw her in this costume. The official photographs made on the day of the coronation of the new queen show her loveliness but also convey her inner joy and her love for the Hungarian people, who in her mind had become identical with Gyula Andrássy. These were hectic days filled with ceremonies which she would have despised at other times, but she did not mind them now.

Ten months after the coronation Elisabeth gave birth to her fourth child, whose father—despite the gossip at the court of Vienna—was doubtless the emperor himself. Before the birth the empress wrote sentimental poems about her gift of a new king for the Hungarian people. She hoped that the dual monarchies of Austria and Hungary would develop along the lines Andrássy intended—with Rudolf as the emperor of Austria and with Hungary under its own king—namely the second son Elisabeth hoped she would bear. It was fitting that Elisabeth gave birth to this child not in Vienna, but in Buda Castle. The child, however, was a girl, and all the political speculations had been in vain—a matter that delighted the non-Hungarians at the Austrian court.

For the old archduchess 1867 was a year of great sorrow: her favorite son, Emperor Maximilian of Mexico, was executed by his enemies in Querétaro. Sophie never recovered from this blow. She died in 1872 and was deeply mourned by Franz Joseph.

Shortly after the tragedy in Mexico, there was an embarrassing meeting of the French and Austrian ruling couples in Salzburg. Everyone knew of the complicity of Napoleon III and particularly that of his beau-

THE IMPERIAL STYLE

tiful wife, Eugénie, in Maximilian's death. The condolence visit in August 1867 therefore caused a furor. The meeting was a drama that caused a political as well as social sensation in Europe.

The two most beautiful royal women of their time were to meet: Eugénie, born countess of Montijo, was now forty-two years old; Elisabeth, queen of Hungary, was twenty-nine. Eugénie dressed simply. She came to the meeting all in white, with a veil before her face and was, despite her age, an elegant, beautiful lady. Archduke Ludwig, the younger brother of the emperor, said of her: "From the first moment she was *ravissante.*... When our own empress kissed Eugénie, she lifted her veil and one saw the still-lovely pastel picture: a short white dress, superb feet and hands. She was totally the *belle femme, mais la très humble servante de la nôtre*, a part she played very deftly and graciously, without losing any of her dignity."

Others, of course, criticized Eugénie's short dress, finding it much too coquettish. Sisi, on the other hand, in a violet-colored floor-length skirt, had been much more tastefully dressed. Elisabeth admired Eugénie's renowned delicate feet. She herself had large, bony hands and extraordinarily large feet, which had become rough from her zealous hiking. Most observers of the scene in Salzburg agreed that the younger lady had not overshadowed the older one in elegance or in regularity of features, but that she had possessed almost ethereal radiance.

Unless official court functions had to do with her beloved Hungary, Elisabeth was absent from them more often than ever. Before the ostentatious court balls in the Hofburg in Vienna she regularly developed what was snidely called "Hofball disease"; she excused herself with headaches or other ailments in order not to have to appear. It is thus understandable that the Viennese society had a poor opinion of its undutiful empress. Every appearance in public was a great sacrifice for her. She complained when she had to hold *cercle* with the ladies at court or make conversation with the dignitaries. She complained of everything that interfered with her freedom. The more patient and permissive the emperor was with her the more self-

centered she became. Her beauty placed her above the rules. Since her public appearances were unexpected and rare, every one of them became a sensational event.

One occasion on which the empress was admired in public was the wedding of her eldest daughter, Archduchess Gisela, to a Bavarian prince in 1873. Elisabeth, then thirty-five, surpassed her seventeen year old and rather plump daughter in beauty and youthful appearance. She wore a silver-embroidered dress in the modern, narrow cut, and her hair was half down, falling to her shoulders and held with a diamond diadem.

The so-called *Gründerzeit* was a time of great luxury in Vienna. A very wasteful life-style coexisted with great poverty. The population of Vienna had doubled in the years between 1840 and 1970, from 440,000 to 900,000. There had been two thousand factories in Vienna in 1850; by 1870 there were forty thousand. There was a desperate shortage of housing for the lower classes. Very often twelve people had to share a room of 115 square feet. A laborer's life expectancy was thirty-three years. While poor people hardly had the means to clothe their children, society ladies frowned on wearing the same dress more than twice and struggled to outdo each other in the display of spectacular jewelry. But no one outdid the empress. Her dresses, her hats, her jewels set the fashion trends in all Europe, just as Empress Eugénie's wardrobe had been emulated ten years earlier in France. (Eugénie went into exile after the revolution in 1871.) Sisi's crown of hair was imitated more often than any other aspect of her appearance. She herself referred to it as her "trademark coiffure." Hardly another woman in Europe had such a mass of hair; most had to rely on hairpieces.

Elisabeth's most successful public appearance on an international level was at the Viennese World Exhibition in 1873. Emperors, kings, and presidents from all over the world came to Vienna, not only to see the pavilions of the exhibition but also to admire Sisi's legendary beauty. The shah of Persia, one of the most exotic and uninhibited guests, made himself most unpopular by trying to put his arm around the very unapproachable empress. This gesture—inspired by sheer admiration—was nearly *lèse-majesté*. That is how much above all others Elisabeth felt herself to be when she was "in harness"—acting in her official court capacity.

On the other hand, Elisabeth had great curiosity about common people. She traveled only incognito—under the name "Countess von Hohenembs." She loved to walk along the Ringstrasse with her large dogs and was very angry if anyone recognized her. Yet her tall, slender figure immediately attracted attention, as did her elegant dresses, her rich jewelry, and her excited ladies.

During the carnival of 1874 she and Ida Ferenczy attended a masked ball in secret. It was the famous "Rudolfinaredoute" on Mardi Gras, which is still held annually in the grand ballroom of the Hofburg. The emperor knew nothing of his wife's escapade. She also deceived her servants by having herself undressed as usual, going to bed, and pretending to sleep—just as in a novel. When her servants had withdrawn, Ida Ferenczy slipped into her room with the fancy-dress costume, a magnificent yellow domino made of heavy brocade. Ida also brought the empress a red blonde wig and a mask with long black tassels that completely covered her face. Ida wore a red domino and was also masked—as is still the custom at the Rudolfinaredoute. The two slipped into the hall and at first only watched the goings-on from the balcony. Elisabeth was fascinated. She had been to every sort of function by then, but never to a masked ball. When she became tired of looking, the empress selected from the crowd a young man who was obviously without an escort. Ida brought him, a government employee in his late twenties, to the masked empress, who spent the rest of the evening in the company of Fritz Pacher. She questioned him about politics, asked whether he was satisfied with the government, inquired what he thought of the empress, and finally talked to him about her favorite poet, Heinrich Heine. She flirted with the young man, but could not be moved to lift her mask by a centimeter. The ball of the yellow domino was followed by a series of letters between the blonde "Gabriele" and Pacher. These letters have survived and confirm the fairy-tale story. More than ten years later Elisabeth wrote a poem called "Long, Long Ago. The Song of the Yellow Domino."

Whether the empress went on other such escapades is not known. It is most likely that this is not the only episode of its kind, yet the only people who could have known about these harmless adventures were Ida Ferenczy and Feifalik, the hairdresser—and perhaps one of Elisabeth's sisters.

The crowning event of the luxurious Viennese *Gründerzeit* was the celebration of the silver anniversary of the emperor and empress in 1879. An enormous parade in honor of the couple took place along the still unfinished Ringstrasse. Everyone wore costumes of the sixteenth century and rode in splendid carriages drawn by marvelously decorated horses. Hans Makart, the most famous painter of his day, designed the costumes. Vienna was the center of the production of historical theater costumes. Even the members of the imperial family, including the crown prince, dressed as "living pictures" for certain events during the celebration. It was, after all, a period of intense historicism. Austria did not develop an artistic style of its own in the late nineteenth century but revived earlier "historical" styles. Even in architecture the past was alive. The new Vienna city hall was resplendent in the Gothic style; the Parliament was conceived in classical Greek style. It was a time when artistic identity was subsumed into the bustle of business and the amassing of wealth. The empress was strangely untouched by all this hectic activity. She did not really embrace the tasteless fashions of the Makart time and was always a trace more elegantly and simply dressed than the other ladies, but she always stood out because of her jewelry and her remarkably slender figure. She complained about the festivities, saying that it was quite enough to be married for twenty-five years and that there was no reason to celebrate. Her sullenness during the official functions surrounding the silver anniversary was quite obvious to all. Vicious slogans were heard at court. It was said, for instance, that the imperial couple was not celebrating twenty-five years of *ménage*, but twenty-five years of manege—a quip about Elisabeth's passion for riding.

*Fig. 110. Christmas in the Hofburg, 1887, a year before Rudolf's suicide. Left to right: Archduchess Marie Valerie; little "Erzi," Rudolf's only child; the imperial couple; Stefanie, Rudolf's wife; and the crown prince. Wood engraving, drawn by Wilhelm Gause. Austrian National Library, Vienna. Inv. no. NB 513.153.*

Fig. 111. Detail of formal
court mourning dress.
Bodice of black satin
trimmed with Chantilly
lace and jet bead embroi-
dery. Not shown: Black
satin skirt with bustle and
train, black lace bonnet,
and black velvet veil-mask
edged with black lace.

The extremely small waist
suggests that the costume
is from the wardrobe
of Empress Elisabeth.
Kunsthistorisches Museum,
Vienna. Photo: Joshua
Greene.

Until 1875 Elisabeth had been satisfied to ride daily in the Prater, to take part in the *parcours* hunts in Bohemia, and above all to ride on the sandy ground of Gödöllö Castle in Hungary. After 1875, however, she went on annual trips to hunt in foreign countries as well—first to France, then to England and Ireland. She was accompanied by about ninety people—good riders, ladies and gentlemen of Viennese and Budapest society, her sisters (particularly Queen Mary of Naples, who had been exiled from her kingdom since 1860)—and naturally by a great many servants and grooms. Elisabeth traveled in a special train with splendidly equipped salon cars. Her luggage—which weighed about forty tons—went by a special freight train.

The emperor was always generous with his beautiful wife. She could spend as much money as she wanted, and she did so with abandon. A six-week sojourn in Ireland, for instance, cost 150,337 florins. In comparison, Crown Prince Rudolf received an annual allowance of 40,000 florins; a professor at the university earned about 2,000 florins a year; a laborer working on the demolition of the old Viennese fortifications made 360 florins a year—for a twelve- to fifteen-hour workday. Women earned about half as much for the same number of hours of work—about 180 florins a year.

Elisabeth spent about three hours each morning—even on her hunting trips—being dressed and having her hair coiffed. For such a trip she took, aside from an imposing number of day and evening dresses, no fewer than sixteen riding habits, and while on a trip always bought new habits in the latest style. She preferred dark blue riding habits and riding hats with small billowing veils.

The empress had herself sewn into her riding habit every morning, and to the dismay of the prudish English aristocracy, she did not wear a petticoat under her habit; her only undergarment was a very soft chemise of finest kid, which was as tight as a second skin. Naturally, she had herself sewn into that every morning too.

The English and Irish newspapers always reported on the elegance of the "empress behind the hounds" (Fig. 109). On one occasion, for instance, she wore a riding habit decorated with gold buttons embossed with the imperial crest and a new narrow-brimmed riding hat. She wore a pin fastened to the white stock in her décolleté and another pin in the form of a clover leaf fastened to her coat. The severe, tight cut of the riding habit underlined her height. Sisi was not only the most beautiful rider, she was also the most daring and courageous. No ditch was too deep, no hurdle too high. She survived several accidents by sheer luck. She had the most skillful riders teach her every finesse of horsemanship. Her favorite "captain" on the hunts in England and Ireland was Bay Middleton, a stocky, red-haired country gentleman who promptly fell in love with the empress, who was his senior by nine years. Elisabeth was not unmoved by Middleton's rough, rather coarse charm. She flirted with him and enjoyed his attention.

The common people adored the beautiful empress, but they saw no more than her tall, slender figure on the most expensive horses in Europe. Her face remained invisible even during the hunts in the 1880s, she always hid behind a little leather fan attached to her saddle. She did this both because she was embarrassed by the curious looks, and because she was vain. Her skin had already become very wrinkled from wind and sun, and Sisi used the fan to preserve the legend of her renowned beauty.

Never before or after were ladies' riding habits as elegant or refined as in the 1880s, when Elisabeth set the pace for the fashion on the *parcours*. Never had riding been as fashionable for ladies of society. The extravagance of his wife's choice of riding habits caused even the good-natured Franz Joseph to ridicule her a little. His comment, when Sisi showed herself in a very ostentatious black and white striped riding habit, was, "Sisi, you look like a zebra!"

The emperor was not the only member of her family to admire Sisi's beauty. Crown Prince Rudolf was also an avid admirer of his mother. That was particularly obvious in 1880, when the empress stopped briefly in Brussels to congratulate her son on his engagement to the Belgian princess Stefanie. Elisabeth met her future daughter-in-law on the platform of the Brussels train station at eight in the morning. Stefanie, a shy sixteen-year-old, who was never to gain Elisabeth's confidence, wore a black dress, white gloves, and a white hat. She was promptly mocked by Elisabeth, who remarked to her Hungarian ladies-in-waiting: "Isn't that the height of tastelessness?" Elisabeth was indisputably the central figure at this confrontation. All who saw her praised her regal appearance. She wore a dark blue dress trimmed with sable and very simply cut to underline her extremely slender figure. Rudolf, who was not altogether happy about his engagement, was the first to notice that his mother overshadowed the Belgian queen as well as the little princess.

In 1881 Elisabeth suddenly gave up her passion for riding. The official reason that a trip to Ireland was cancelled was an attack of sciatica. The true reason may have been that Bay Middleton could not act as her escort on that hunt. Without him, and with the realization that at forty-four she could no longer keep up with the younger riders, she lost her pleasure in riding. If she could not be the first in something—could not be the center of attention—she turned to another passion.

With no less intensity she now took up fencing. When she had mastered that after hours of daily practice, she turned to swimming and then to hiking. She seemed compelled to be in constant motion; she would walk—run, really—every day in rain or shine through the Wienerwald or through the Bavarian mountains. Even her personal yacht, the *Miramare*, was designed so that she could take extensive hikes every day. Her ladies-in-waiting, who had to accompany her, fainted from exhaustion or suffered from foot problems. The first prerequisite for a lady-in-waiting of the empress was to be athletic. Elisabeth liked to take her large dogs—her Scottish whippet, "Horseguard," or the blue gray Great Dane, "Shadow," with her on her hikes. She once remarked, "I think a dog as large as I would like simply does not exist."

The empress forgot about fashion on her hikes. She usually wore a simple ankle-length dark skirt, a blouse, and a dark, tailored coat. This forerunner of the suit was cut like a riding habit. No matter how bad the weather, Elisabeth never stayed indoors. She always took along a waterproof coat and was well equipped with galoshes and an enormous umbrella. Her shoes were stout and clumsy. In the city she wore the simplified "English" black leather shoes with very low heels. These became popular—at least with the middle class—because of her. Franz Joseph viewed his wife's unusual activities with incomprehension, but with generosity. He never complained when she left him to fulfill their official obligations alone. He accepted her fanatical riding, as he did her fencing, her hiking, and finally her poetry.

Elisabeth had started writing poems as a young girl. Throughout her life she read avidly, which was unusual for a lady in her social position. Her favorite writers were Shakespeare, Shelley, Byron, and, above all, Heinrich Heine. She felt particular empathy with Heine, who faced so much strife as part of the anti-semitism rife in the nineteenth century. Elisabeth tried to imitate his style and even imagined that her adored master dictated poems to her. She wrote hundreds of poems in his style; many of these are jibes at Viennese society.

Sisi retreated into her Weltschmerz through her own and Heine's writings. Nothing inspired her except her daughter Valerie. Even Andrássy and his ambition to return to politics in the 1880s did not interest her. She never again took an active part in matters of state.

It was not love that tied Elisabeth to Franz Joseph, but his loneliness moved her. In 1888 she did something that seems "progressive" even today: she saw to it that he found a "friend," the actress Katharina Schratt. It was Elisabeth who introduced the two and who made sure that their friendship was openly tolerated and did not cause a scandal. The emperor was eternally grateful to his wife for her generosity in this matter.

Elisabeth took no interest in her only son, Rudolf. The intelligent crown prince also wrote in secret—not poetry like his mother, but stinging political articles for the liberal newspaper *Neues Wiener Tagblatt*. Rudolf was caught up in an unhappy marriage, isolated from his family at the court of Vienna, and was suffering from an apparently incurable disease. He vehemently opposed his father's political ideology and turned to desperate political activities to demonstrate his position. He would have liked to be close to his mother, whose beliefs and viewpoints he had always tried to imitate through his own antiaristocratic and liberal stance, but he received no recognition from Elisabeth. Only for Valerie, her "only one," did the empress rouse herself from her egotistical dreams.

The tragedy of Mayerling, which took place on January 30, 1889, caught Elisabeth completely unprepared. It was she who received the most loving farewell letter from the crown prince before his suicide. Franz Joseph got no word of farewell from his son. Only after the thirty-year-old Rudolf and his seventeen-year-old mistress were dead did Elisabeth recognize her spiritual rapport with her son. She began a cult of the dead for Rudolf. The foreign press reported that the empress of Austria had gone mad after Mayerling. That was an exaggeration, but although she was to live on for almost ten more years, Elisabeth did make her final reckoning with life after Rudolf's death. She gave away all her beautiful clothes and most of her jewelry (which the recipients returned to her secretly). After January 30, 1889, she wore only black and took no interest in her wardrobe. The trends in Viennese fashion were now set by Countess Pauline Metternich, whose penchant for the flamboyant plumed hats of the Makart time, an abundance of plush, and heavy makeup always drew sarcastic remarks from Elisabeth. She herself became a walking *mater dolorosa*, who roused not pity, but ridicule, especially from the Viennese aristocracy.

Elisabeth rarely appeared in Vienna. She wandered through Europe, particularly Greece, to remote unpopular places, in the company of scholars and others, who read Greek to her. Her traveling costume was always the same: a black suit, interchangeable little black hats, and a fan or an umbrella to hide her wrinkled face. She now learned ancient and modern Greek and made the Greek heroes of antiquity her idols; Achilles was her favorite. For hours on end, young Greek scholars would read aloud to her as she hiked. She practiced her Greek by translating *Hamlet* and *King Lear* from English into modern Greek. Her favorite play remained *A Midsummer Night's Dream*. In her poems she imagined herself to be Titania, Franz Joseph to be King Oberon, and one or another admirer

from the past (like Bay Middleton) to be the donkey.

Elisabeth loved the sea and stormy weather. At one time she fantasized drowning in a storm at sea. Her morbid fantasies grew more and more intense. She spoke with the deceased King Ludwig II of Bavaria, with her dead son, and repeatedly with her "master," Heinrich Heine.

Death came to Elisabeth at sixty. For more than ten years she had not allowed hope or plans to enter her life, nor had she authorized any pictures to be taken of her (Fig. 112). Her life had ended with Rudolf's. She had kept her tall, slender figure through constant dieting, which made her look youthful from a distance, but gave her a bad complexion, a listless eye, and hunger edema over her entire body. Her cold-water baths had irritated the rheumatism she had begun to suffer. She knew that she had become ugly. Her assassin, a young anarchist who stabbed her with a ratchet on the shore of Lake Geneva, ended the restless wanderings of the tormented empress. Her favorite lines of poetry were by Lord Byron:

*Count o'er the joys thine hours have seen.*
*Count o'er the days from anguish free,*
*And know, whatever thou has been*
*T'is something better not to be!*

# The Wiener Werkstätte

By Ursula Kehlmann, Director of the Austrian
Fashion Center, Vienna, with assistance from Lucie
Hampel, Curator of the Costume Collection, Schloss
Hetzendorf, Museen der Stadt Wien

The Secessionist movement at the turn of the twentieth century heralded an era in Viennese art that was to
have long-lasting international repercussions. The
Secessionists, led by the painter Gustav Klimt and
based at the Austrian Museum for Art and Industry and
the School for Applied Arts, wanted to reform the concept of industrial design, to replace shoddy, ill-con-
ceived merchandise with practical, well-made forms.
Many of the fundamental aesthetic ideas of the twentieth century were formulated by the Viennese group,
which was inspired by the Arts and Crafts movement in
England. The mixture of the English ideas and the particular purity and ardor of the Viennese artists' thinking
resulted in the founding of the Wiener Werkstätte
("Vienna Workshop") in May 1903. Wilhelm Mrazek
writes that in that month

> the young industrialist and art lover Fritz
> Wärndorfer returned from one of his many trips to
> England and met with two of his artist friends,
> Josef Hoffmann and Koloman Moser, at their
> favorite café. Arts and crafts in England and
> Vienna was the subject under discussion. Moser
> talked about his desire for a community of artists
> and craftsmen like the one [Charles Robert]
> Ashbee had founded in England. Wärndorfer, who
> was enthusiastic about the English movement,
> declared that he was prepared to put up the capital
> necessary to get the project under way. A few days
> later headquarters had been found and three sym-
> pathetic craftsmen had been hired. In June the
> undertaking was officially constituted as the Wie-
> ner Werkstätte Produktiv Gemeinschaft von
> Kunsthandwerkern in Wien [the Vienna Work-
> shop Productive Association of Artisans in
> Vienna]. Fritz Wärndorfer took over the manage-
> ment of the finances; Hoffmann and Moser func-
> tioned as the artistic directors. Their bustling ate-
> lier soon outgrew its quarters, and in the fall of
> 1903 the Wiener Werkstätte moved to a new studio
> at no. 32 Neustiftgasse in the seventh district of
> the city.

The first catalogue of Wiener Werkstätte products
was published in 1905. It contained a statement of pur-
pose, probably jointly written by Hoffmann and Moser.
In its language and content, the following excerpt from
that manifesto conveys the enthusiasm and sense of
beginning the young artists felt:

> The unlimited damage caused by ugly mass-pro-
> duced goods and careless imitation of old styles
> deluges our lives. We have lost our connection
> with the arts of the past and are tossed about by a
> thousand conflicting attitudes. The machine has
> replaced the hand; the businessman has replaced
> the artisan. To swim against the current would
> seem to be madness.
>
> Yet we have founded our workshop. It will be a
> center of gravity on our native soil resounding with
> the happy clangor of arts and crafts, and will be
> open to all who acknowledge Ruskin and Morris.
> We want to establish rapport among the public,
> the designer, and the artisan. We turn for support
> to all who value culture in the true sense and hope
> that our friends will not be dismayed by the mis-
> takes we must inevitably make as we fumble
> toward our goals.
>
> Our first priority is function. Every object we
> make must display good proportions and the best
> use of materials. We will use decoration where it is
> appropriate, but not as a matter of course. We will
> use many semiprecious stones, particularly for
> jewelry; because of their vivid colors and almost
> infinite variety, they will replace diamonds in our
> work. We love silver and gold for their luster, but
> to us copper has the same artistic merits. We
> acknowledge that jewelry made of gold and pre-
> cious stones has value, but we feel that an artisan's
> work in any medium should be judged by the same
> standards applied to the work of all artists.
>
> We cannot and do not want to compete with
> cheap products that degrade the craftsman. Our
> foremost aim is to give the craftsman satisfaction in
> his skills and to make work with dignity possible
> for him, a goal we must approach step by step.

In 1908 the work of the best Viennese couturiers was
honored in a "Jubilee Exhibition of Viennese Fashion."
Many of the artists whose work was shown there were
employed by the Wiener Werkstätte after 1912, when
fashions were included in the workshop's output.

The unique social structure of imperial Vienna at the
turn of the century created the climate in which the
Wiener Werkstätte could thrive. Twelve nations were

ruled from Vienna through an intricate administrative bureaucracy. The civil servants who operated the system formed the bourgeoisie. The aristocracy, conservative and reserved, lived a self-contained life on their estates and returned to Vienna only for the social season. The ladies ordered their gowns from the couture houses of Drecoll, Spitzer, and Grünbaum, who followed the latest Parisian trends. Or dresses might be ordered from the approved court dressmakers.

Middle- and high-ranking civil servants, who were as reserved as their betters, dressed in unobtrusive ready-made clothes from the renowned houses of Zwieback, Gerngross, and Herzmansky. Special orders were filled by the smaller couture salons.

The Wiener Werkstätte dressed a segment of the population not catered to by the other couture houses. The first wave of industrialization in Austria had created a new grand bourgeoisie. This newly monied class, deeply committed to cultural affairs and considering patronage of the arts its natural duty, formed the first Viennese avant-garde.

Among members of this class a new intellectual life came into being. Discussion groups were formed, and people of like minds gathered in cafés to exchange ideas. Soon the homes of certain outstanding women replaced the cafés as gathering places. As Milan Dubrovic has written in his biography of Berta Zuckerkandl:

The literary bourgeoisie—industrialists, engineers, doctors, painters, writers, and musicians—met in these salons, in which certain ambitious hostesses held court. The homes of Josephine von Wertheimstein and the singer Karoline Bettelheim (wife of the industrialist Julius Gomperz) were two such cultural centers.

Alma Mahler-Werfel and the teacher Xenia Schwarzwald also achieved prominence. Berta Zuckerkandl [Fig. 113], known as the "Hofrätin" [the "privy councillor"],was a particularly ardent devotée of the new ideas—especially those having to do with the creative arts—which she defended and propagated with zeal. As the author of countless newspaper articles, she inspired and organized many others. She may have inherited her fighting spirit, which she used to support the ideas of her protegés, from her father, Morris Szeps, a noted journalist, the founder of the liberal daily *Wiener Tagblatt*, and an adviser and confidant to Crown Prince Rudolf. Berta's brother, Julius Szeps, was the editor in chief of the respected newspaper *Wiener Allgemeinen Zeitung;* her husband was the famous physician Hofrat Emil Zuckerkandl, and her sister was married to Paul Clemenceau, brother of the French statesman Georges Clemenceau ("the Tiger").

The list of her illustrious family connections not only demonstrates Zuckerkandl's social standing, but also identifies her as an active member of the intellectual bourgeoisie, which in the early years of the century still had unquenchable optimism and an unshakable faith in progress.

Zuckerkandl had been swept up early on in the revolutionary atmosphere that permeated Viennese society at the turn of the century. Among her adherents were the major revolutionaries of the world of art and architecture: Otto Wagner and Josef Hoffmann, the painters Klimt, Kokoschka, and Schiele, and the composer Schönberg. She was a defender of Sigmund Freud and an early promoter of the playwright Arthur Schnitzler, whose father, Professor Johann Schnitzler, had founded the Vienna Polyclinic and was a colleague of Emil Zuckerkandl. Through Schnitzler Berta Zuckerkandl came into contact with Hugo von Hofmannsthal, Hermann Bahr, Richard Beer-Hoffmann, and Peter Altenberg. Her special love was the theater, and she translated no fewer than 120 plays into German from the French.

The "Hofrätin," or "Aunt Berta," as she was called by her friends, was a brilliant hostess. On Sunday afternoons in her home at no. 6 Oppolzergasse, overlooking the Ringstrasse, she received the leading practitioners of Viennese culture and politics.

The new interest in beauty and refinement as a way of life brought women into the center of attention in a unique way. Many women, like Berta Zuckerkandl, already perceived emancipation as a matter of course and took a role in society equal to a man's.

Arthur Schnitzler's play *Anatol* is a tribute to the women of his time and gives us a glimpse into the struc-

ture of the Viennese society at the turn of the century. Christine, the lady of the world, typifies the intellectual of the new society. At the opposite pole is the sweet girl of the lower middle class, who had been a recognized type in Viennese art and literature since the Biedermeier period.

The ideas of the artis couturiers of the Wiener Werkstätte coincided with the new feminism. Their unstructured designs underlined the liberal attitudes and were executed with a care and detail that showed an all-encompassing respect for materials and workmanship (Fig. 114).

When Paul Poiret came to Vienna in 1913 to visit the artists he had met at the World's Exposition in Rome the year before, it was Berta Zuckerkandl who introduced him to Hoffmann and Klimt and their set. As she herself said of the encounter, "Very soon the close connections between the style of Poiret and that of the Klimt group became obvious.... Through Paul Poiret the Austrian taste was once again brought into contact with the French tradition."

Portraits of women of this time—paintings by Kees van Dongen in Paris (Fig. 115) and by Klimt in Vienna (Fig. 116)—attest the strong differences between the styles of the women in these two centers. The society women van Dongen depicted are modish and almost playful; Klimt's women are intellectual and self-assured.

The architect Eduard Josef Wimmer became the first head of the fashion division of the Wiener Werkstätte (Fig. 117). Wimmer felt himself very much in accord with his clients of the grand new bourgeoisie. His aesthetic sensibility and his empathy made it possible for him to interpret architectural lines, forms, and ornaments in terms of fashion. In Wimmer's designs, the linearity, the fantasy of the silhouette, always complemented the character of the wearer and served to underline her allure. Ornamentation might or might not be used—but it was always secondary to form.

With the inauguration of the fashion branch of the workshop, it was necessary to start a dressmaking atelier. Except for the dresses made at the salon of the Flöge sisters (Fig. 118), who identified themselves with

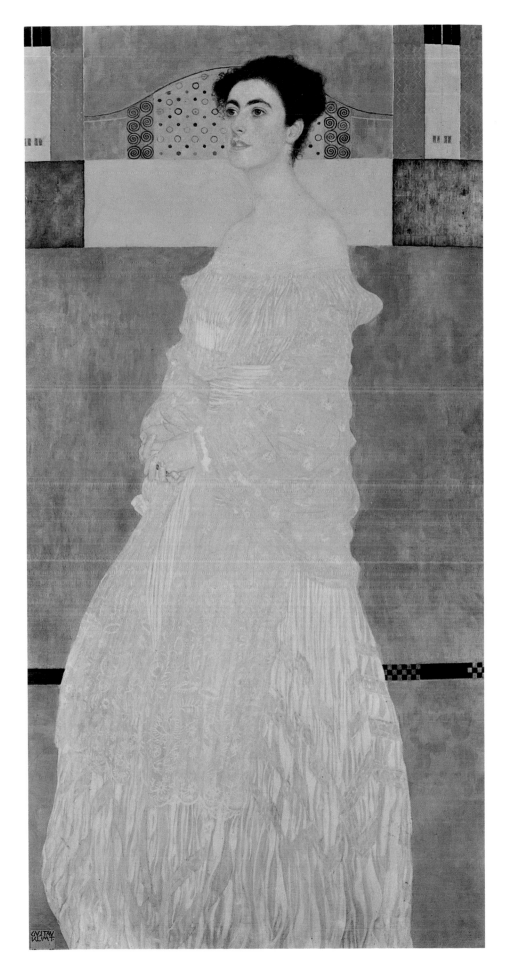

*Figs. 117. Three designs
by Eduard Wimmer, 1912.
Austrian Museum for
Applied Arts, Vienna.*

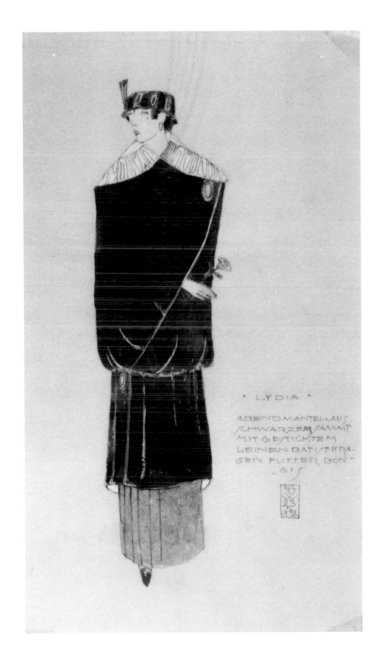

* LYDIA *

ABEND MANTEL AUS
SCHWARZEM SAMMT
MIT GESTICKTEM
LEINEN BATIST KRA-
GEN FUTTER BON-
GIS

the Wiener Werkstätte, all the designs that bore the workshop label were made on the premises. The first fashion collection was shown in 1913 in Berlin. A review in the *Neuen Stettiner Zeitung* declared: "...There is nothing contrived about this art of fashion. It is a question of sensibility carried by sensitivity for harmony of color and line." As another journalist wrote, "Wimmer's Viennese ladies don't lose their quality of charm even under the most ostentatious robes." Berta Zuckerkandl published the following assessment of the Wiener Werkstätte's achievement in the *Wiener Allgemeinen Zeitung:*

> The Romans made the first practical yet beautiful clothes for women. Later the French developed the hip-enveloping corset, which constricted all the internal organs but created a streamline silhouette. The sack dress is a twentieth-century revival of the Empire style, yet it is governed by an entirely new aesthetic, with freedom of movement its most important priority. The physical freedom of movement and the social freedom it represented were embodied in the lady's suit.
>
> It was logical that the spirit of the Klimt group should lead to the creation of the Wiener Werkstätte dress. The leading artists of Vienna have raised the frippery of fashion to a noble craft. They have even created outstanding fabrics, unique in color and ornamentation, for their original designs. They have utterly changed the concept of accessories through the batik sashes, hand embroideries, wool crocheting, silk flowers, knitted belts, and novel passementerie. They have taught us to realize that design determines the character of the dress. These dresses, coats, sashes, and hats work because they are decorative distillations of an idea of our time. Through careful, conscious design, fashion has become a style.

Poiret meanwhile has made his own radical experiments in the aesthetic of women's fashions. When he saw the Klimt room at the World Exposition in Rome he sensed a remarkable harmony between Parisian and Viennese designs. But only after one sees the Poiret dresses beside the Viennese styles does one realize the power of the Viennese clothes. As paradoxical as it may seem, it was only through comparison with the world-famous

Poiret styles that the Wiener Werkstätte styles became popular.

Viennese fabrics were sent to Paris, and for the first time since the glorious days of the Congress of Vienna Viennese fashion set trends in the world market. The fashion show arranged by the architect Eduard Wimmer at the invitation of the house of Friedmann and Weber in Berlin was as crowded as the Poiret show had been. The same kind of show is taking place simultaneously in Cologne and Düsseldorf; requests have even come from London for Wiener Werkstätte designs. Their popularity is due to their being such accurate reflections of the art of their time. Gradually exposure to this refined style will spawn a class of women who demand it; a higher cultural level will naturally produce a more refined sense of fashion design.

The original concept developed by Josef Hoffmann and Koloman Moser—a principle of design based on the geometric abstraction of the square—was also the basis for the Wiener Werkstätte fashions. The decorative fabrics designed by such artists as Dagobert Peche, Maria Likarz, Felicie and Kitty Rix, Mathilde Flöge, and Wimmer's associate Max Snischek were the starting point for the workshop's couture creations. The designs in the first Wiener Werkstätte fashion collection were made for the most part by Wimmer himself and by Max Snischek. The first collection included not only day and evening clothes; the designers experimented on themselves and their friends by creating housedresses and negligées. Two of the earliest Wiener Werkstätte designs were work smocks for Klimt and the sculptor Anton Hanack. The designers wanted to create clothes that were both useful and beautiful. Hoffmann even wanted to make fashions that complemented the room in which they were worn. The total concept of a dress was considered, down to the details of pearl embroidery by Maria Likarz.

In 1928 in honor of the twenty-fifth anniversary of the founding of the Wiener Werkstätte, the journal *Deutsche Kunst und Dekoration* printed the following article. Here Josef Hoffmann sets forth simply and precisely the goals, duties, and achievements of the Wiener Werkstätte since its creation:

THE IMPERIAL STYLE

## Our Road to Humanity

The Wiener Werkstätte, which was founded in 1903, is an undertaking that furthers and nurtures all artistic and qualitative endeavors in the field of modern craftsmanship. The workshop has its own studios, with a group of excellent craftsmen and artisans at work in almost every area of the arts and crafts. These people produce the things the world knows and demands as the outstanding products of the Wiener Werkstätte. Since the designer is in constant contact with the workshop and sees his projects through all phases of production, his products are of a superlative quality one doesn't otherwise find being made today. It is our custom to sign our products, which may also increase their value.

Our studios include workshops for silver, gold, metal, tin, and enameling, for leather goods and book covers, for fashion and knitwear, pearl beading, embroidery, fabric painting, and for all types of ceramics. Woven and printed fabrics, carpets, wallpaper, and printed silks are produced in outstanding factories associated with our organization. Laces and special knitted detail work are commissioned from craftswomen who produce it at home with the greatest care and attention. We do not shun machine work where it is practical and carefully done, but we use it only on our largest productions. We work from conception to completion and will not tolerate an incomplete initial drawing. The enamels, metalworking, and most of the ceramics are finished by the artists who designed them. All ceramics, even figural pieces, are made and fired in the workshop. The fashion department makes only its own designs, which is unique for any atelier outside Paris.

Our main achievement has been to give practical and appropriate forms to all objects and then to make these unique and valuable through pleasing proportions and harmonious shapes. The materials, the tools, and sometimes the machine are our only means of expression. We do not dictate to an artist, but seek only to encourage him to follow his own intuition and develop his creative power.

We follow the same working methods artists have used in all truly creative periods of history. The idea of accepting a style without building on it and making it one's own leads to stagnation and decline. We are reacting to this unwholesome artistic atmosphere, which has recently been current in Europe. We believe in looking back to a healthy tradition—for instance, the Empire style—drawing inspiration from it, and creating new forms. Mere copying, no matter how well done, is always worthless and can never replace an original. A piece of copied work will always betray its origins and seem like a mask because it is not a true product of its time. At the Wiener Werkstätte we have achieved fresh and modern perceptions; our fashions, our cars, our ships have been made in forms that reflect a modern aesthetic. It is natural that as a result of our work the search is on for new forms in every field.

We want our work to be in step with our philosophy, and yet we hope never to thwart the individual artist who is inspired to express himself. We stand on the growing edge of art and design in Europe and ask understanding and encouragement from all enlightened people.

The Wiener Werkstätte was in financial trouble from the start, despite the support of Fritz Wärndorfer. The artists' demand for quality was of course very expensive. In 1913 Wärndorfer realized that his capital, which had come from the family cotton spinnery in Bohemia, was exhausted. The banker Otto Primavesi, who had long been a friend of Klimt and Hoffmann, took over the role of patron and financial manager of the organization.

The level of production at the workshop dropped after the outbreak of World War I, which brought on devastating changes in society and severe economic crises. Further, the artists of the Wiener Werkstätte had found a bitter enemy in Adolf Loos, an architect who attacked their beliefs in his works and through his publications. His austere, sober concept of design stood in opposition to everything Josef Hoffmann and his circle had been trying to achieve.

The war had the effect of liberating people from many established conventions, and afterward fashion too became separated from its social context. On the Wiener Werkstätte fashions made after the war orna-

Fig. 119. Design for a
peasant-style dress by
Fritzi Löw, 1914–15.
Museen der Stadt Wien.
Inv. no. 115.005/1B.

mentation became more prominent; these late designs were on the whole more decorative and self-indulgent (Fig. 120). The economic situation in Austria and the upheaval of the social structure hastened bankruptcy for the Wiener Werkstätte in 1926 and the final closing of the workshops in 1932. The decline of the grand bourgeoisie and the flight of many friends and sponsors meant the end of the workshop's stimulus and guiding spirit.

Only a few of the original Wiener Werkstätte artisans remained in Austria. Gertrude Höchsmann, who had been a student of Hoffmann and a worker at the Wiener Werkstätte, opened a couture salon in Vienna, where she practiced the original concept of pure lines and excellent craftsmanship.

Eduard Wimmer continued to teach and to pass on his concept of design to his students. In 1918 he took over the fashion design class at the School for Applied Arts, where he remained a professor until 1955. He trained many young designers; the works of Federico de Bercéviczy-Pallavicini, who continues Wimmer's tradition, have already entered the collections of many of the greatest museums and connoisseurs. Many ideas that began with the Wiener Werkstätte affect current Viennese fashions and those in many other countries, including the United States.

*Fig. 120. Wiener Werkstätte
evening dress. Black
georgette with cape sleeves
that form floating panels
in the back. Embroidered
with gold beads in ran-
domly placed geometric
shapes. Designed by
Eduard Wimmer, 1920–25.
Austrian Museum of
Applied Arts, Vienna.
Photo: Joshua Greene.*

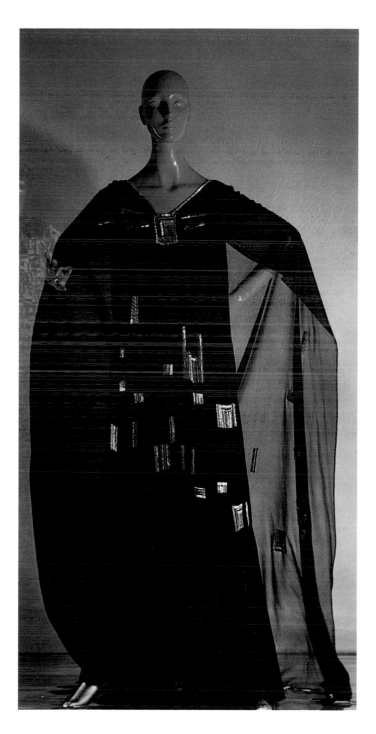

THE IMPERIAL STYLE

# Selected Bibliography

Boehm, Max von. *Bekleidungskunst und Mode.* Munich, 1918.

Boucher, François. *20,000 Years of Fashion.* New York, n.d.

Brabourne, Fourth Baron. *The Political Evolution of the Hungarian Nation.* 2 vols. London, 1908.

Braun-Ronsdorf, Margarete. *Modische Eleganz, Europäische Kostümgeschichte von 1789 bis 1929.* Munich and Vienna, 1970.

Buchsbaum, Maria. *Ferdinand Georg Waldmüller (1793-1865).* Salzburg, 1976.

Corti, Count Egon. *Elisabeth, Empress of Austria.* New Haven, Conn., 1936.

Dubrovic, Milan. *Die Hofrätin Berta Zuckerkandl.* Vienna, n.d.

*Fasching in Wien: Der Wiener Walzer 1750-1850,* exhibition catalogue. Museen der Stadt Wien. Vienna, 1978.

Guest, Ivor. *Fanny Elssler.* Middletown, Conn., 1970.

Halsband, Robert, ed. *The Complete Letters of Lady Mary Wortley Montagu.* 3 vols. Oxford, 1966.

Hampel, Lucie. "Die Mode der Zeit." *Maria Theresia und ihre Zeit,* edited by Walter Koschatsky. Salzburg, 1979.

Hoffmann, Josef, and Moser, Koloman. *Arbeitsprogramm der Wiener Werkstätte.* Vienna, 1905.

Hoffmann, Josef. "Unser Weg zum Menschentum." *Deutsche Kunst und Dekoration* LXII, 1928.

Hürlimann, Martin. *Vienna.* New York, 1970.

Kaut, Hubert. *Modeblätter aus Wien: Mode und Tracht von 1770 bis 1914.* Vienna and Munich, 1970.

Kees, Edler von St. *Fabriks- und Gewerbewesen im Kaiserstaat Österreich.* Vienna, 1823.

Leiter, F. "Die Männer Kleidererzeugung in Wien." *Schriften des Vereins f. Sozialpolitik* 71 (1897), p. 491 f.

Leitich, Ann Tizia. *Verklungenes Wien.* Vienna, 1942.

——————. *Wiener Biedermeier.* Leipzig, 1941.

——————. *Die Wienerin.* Vienna, n.d.

Macartney, C. A. *The Habsburg Empire, 1790-1918.* New York, 1969.

Mattes, Ute. "Die Wiener Mode von 1816-1848." Dissertation, Vienna, 1977.

*Mode-Ausstellung im K. K. Österreichischen Museum für Kunst und Industrie,* exhibition catalogue. Vienna, 1915-16. (Introduction by F. Tilgher.)

Mrazek, Wilhelm. *Die Wiener Werkstätte,* exhibition catalogue. Austrian Museum for Applied Arts. Vienna, 1967.

Parwy, Marcel. *Johann Strauss.* Vienna, 1975.

Perfal, Jost, ed. *Wien Chronik.* Salzburg, 1961.

Schönholz, F. A. von. *Tradition zur Charakteristik Österreichs, seines Staats- und Volkslebens unter Franz I.* Munich, 1914.

Seiter, D. "Die Mode als publizistischer Faktor im Kommunikationsprozess, eine Untersuchung der 'Wiener Moden Zeitung' des 'Repository of Arts' und des 'Journal des Dames et Modes,' 1816-1830." Dissertation, Vienna, 1972.

Slokar, J. *Geschichte der österreichischen Industrie und ihrer Förderung unter Kaiser Franz I.* Vienna, 1972.

Speil, Hilde. *Der Wiener Kongress in Augenzeugenberichten.* Düsseldorf, 1966.

Springschitz, Leopoldine. *Wiener Mode im Wandel der Zeit.* Vienna, 1949.

Thiel, Erika. *Geschichte des Kostüms.* Berlin, 1960.

Tietze, Hans. *Das Vormärzliche Wien in Wort und Bild.* Vienna, 1925.

*200 Jahre Mode in Wien, 1776-1976,* exhibition catalogue. Museen der Stadt Wien. Vienna, 1976.

*Vienna in the Age of Schubert*, exhibition catalogue. Victoria and Albert Museum. London, 1979.

Wagner, R. *Geschichte der Kleiderarbeiter in Österreich im 19. Jahrhundert u. ersten Viertel d. 20. Jahrhunderts*. Vienna, 1930.

Wechsberg, Joseph. *The Waltz Emperors: The Life and Times and Music of the Strauss Family*. London, 1973.

*Wiener Theater des Biedermeier und Vormärz*, exhibition catalogue. Austrian Museum of the Theater. Vienna, 1978.

Zöllner, Erich. *Geschichte Österreichs*. Vienna, 1974.

"Waltz Interlude" is excerpted from an article titled "The Egalitarian Waltz," by Ruth Katz, first published in *Human Nature* and reprinted by permission of the publisher.

We are grateful to the following institutions for permission to reproduce illustrations of works in their collections. Museen der Stadt Wien: Figs. 1, 14–20, 33, 35, 37–40, 42, 43, 71, 73, 74–76, 103, 118, 119. Austrian National Library, Vienna: Figs. 5, 13, 30, 45, 104, 105, 108–110, 112, 113, 117. Österreichische Galerie, Vienna: Figs. 12, 29. Kunsthistorisches Museum, Vienna: Figs. 25, 61, 64, 78–83, 86, 89, 92–94, 96, 97, 100, 101, 106, 107. The Frick Collection, New York: Fig. 34. Hungarian National Museum, Budapest: Figs. 46–50, 52, 55–57. Hungarian Museum of Applied Arts, Budapest: Fig. 53. Museum of Military History, Vienna: Fig. 77. Bayerische Staatsgemälde-sammlungen (Neue Pinakothek), Munich: Fig. 116.

Stylist for photographer Joshua Greene: Vanessa Murphy
Assistant to designer: Adrienne Burk
Composition by Typographic Images, Inc., New York
Printed by Eastern Press, New Haven, Connecticut
Bound by Publishers Book Bindery, Inc.,
Long Island City, New York
Map and line drawings by Joseph P. Ascherl